Foundation Flash Catalyst

Greg Goralski

LordAlex Leon

friendsof

DESIGNER TO DESIGNER™

an Apress® company

Foundation Flash Catalyst

ISBN-13 (pbk): 978-1-4302-2862-2

ISBN-13 (electronic): 978-1-4302-2863-9

Printed and bound in the United States of America 9 8 7 6 5 4 3 2 1

Distributed to the book trade worldwide by Springer Science+Business Media LLC., 233 Spring Street, 6th Floor, New York, NY 10013. Phone 1-800-SPRINGER, fax (201) 348-4505, e-mail orders-ny@springer-sbm.com, or visit www.springeronline.com.

For information on translations, please e-mail rights@apress.com or visit www.apress.com.

Apress and friends of ED books may be purchased in bulk for academic, corporate, or promotional use. eBook versions and licenses are also available for most titles. For more information, reference our Special Bulk Sales–eBook Licensing web page at www.apress.com/info/bulksales.

The source code for this book is freely available to readers at www.friendsofed.com in the Downloads section.

Credits

To my students: you are my source of insight, inspiration, and great new music. Through your eyes, I get to rediscover and get excited about digital media every September.

—Greg Goralski

I dedicate this book to my readers, friends, and family, especially my lovely wife and daughter for their patience, support, and encouragement.

—LordAlex Leon

Contents at a Glance

Contents

Contents

About the Authors

As a professor of interactive media at Humber College, I get to spend my time training and being inspired by the next generation of interactive designers and developers. Over the past few years, I've co-developed IN_situ, an award-winning interactive architectural visualization tool, co-authored the book *Flex for Designers*, and represented Canada as a speaker at Expo in Nagoya Japan on the subject of interactive media innovation. I am honored to hold the National Post Design Exchange Gold Award in the Digital category.

More recently, I added an MBA to my tool set and have been undertaking a critical examination of the business side of our innovative and creative industry.

Greg Goralski

I am a creative technologist specializing in the Flash Platform, an entrepreneur, an author, a blogger, a speaker, an active member of the Flash Platform Community, a geek, and a big fan of science fiction. As founder and chief evangelist forLordAlex Works (LAW), with over 10+ years of experience creating content and compelling user experiences for the internet and devices, I help companies and organizations to plan, execute, and launch their ideas into reality.

I co-authored *Flex for Designers* and *Foundation Adobe Flash Catalyst*, aiming at helping designers and developers work together, create great visual experiences, and create compelling applications, prototypes, and interactions using the Flash Platform. As a blogger since 2002, I've shared my passion and experiences for the Web with thousands of people. I've earned multiple mentions in Internet articles and most recently was mentioned as one the top 50 Flash developers to follow on Twitter.

I am an Adobe Community Professional as well as the Adobe user group manager in Montreal, the largest bilingual Adobe UG (swfMontreal) in Quebec. I also like foreign languages: I am fluent in English, French, and Spanish and am currently learning Russian and Japanese.

LordAlex Leon

About the Technical Reviewers

Josh Freeney is currently a partner in a new Michigan-based interactive firm called YETi CGI. His focus at YETi is getting high-quality Flash content and infrastructure in place to serve both business and entertainment applications. He is also an instructor for the Digital Animation and Game Design program at Ferris State University in Grand Rapids, Michigan. Josh teaches Flash game development classes focused on rapid agile production with maximum reusability. He likes board games, camping, sleeping in, and anything LEGO.

Louis DiCarro is a long-time developer for the Internet and has been working with Flash since version 1. He has taught Flash and ActionScript at several college-level schools for a number of years and is currently a consultant in New York City. In addition to ActionScript developement, he also works in front- and back-end development and likes to play on servers. He is a regular contributor for *Flash and Flex Developer* magazine. Robots of all sorts give him the warm fuzzies.

About the Cover Image Designer

Corné van Dooren designed the front cover image for this book. After taking a brief from friends of ED to create a new design for the *Foundation* series, he worked at combining technological and organic forms, with the results now appearing on this and other books' covers.

Corné spent his childhood drawing on everything at hand and then began exploring the infinite world of multimedia—and his journey of discovery hasn't stopped since. His mantra has always been "The only limit to multimedia is the imagination," a saying that keeps him moving forward constantly.

Corné works for many international clients, writes features for multimedia magazines, reviews and tests software, authors multimedia studies, and works on many other friends of ED books. You can see more of his work at and contact him through his web site, www.cornevandooren.com.

If you like Corné's work, be sure to check out his chapter in *New Masters of Photoshop: Volume 2* (friends of ED, 2004).

Acknowledgments

Special thanks to: Pamela Del Hierro, Bolo Michelin, Dan Loaiza, Dee Sandler, Lee Sutton, Gustavo Brady, Saravana Muthu, Stacey Mulcahy, and Mark Anders.

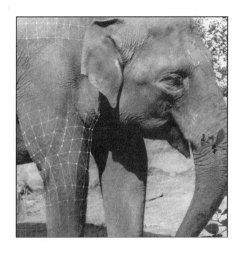

Chapter 1

Catalyst Interface

What we'll cover in this chapter:

- Pages/States panel
- Library and Layers panels
- Properties and Timelines panels

Files used in this chapter:

- None

Introduction to Catalyst

Flash Catalyst is a unique addition to the design tools created by Adobe. It allows a user-interface designer to quickly create an interactive and dynamic prototype of a site that can then be taken into Flash Builder to be completed. You can bring together visual assets created in Illustrator, Photoshop, and Fireworks and add interaction and movement to them. This gives you fine control over how the interface responds to the user's interactions before a developer needs to get involved; it also increases the speed at which an interface can be created and tested and allows for a more iterative design process.

As you create the interface's interactions and movements, the code that drives them is automatically created in the background. The developer can use this code to create the final product in Flash Builder. The naming and structure that are created in Catalyst are also carried along and so need to be well organized. Chapter 6 looks at this topic in depth.

This chapter walks through the elements of the Catalyst interface to give you an initial foundation in the tools and techniques that make up the Catalyst workflow. You use each major section of the interface in your first sample project in Chapter 2; subsequent chapters elaborate on these interface components.

To begin exploring the Catalyst interface, open Flash Catalyst. In the initial dialog box, select Adobe Flash Catalyst Project under the Create New Project heading (see Figure 1-1).

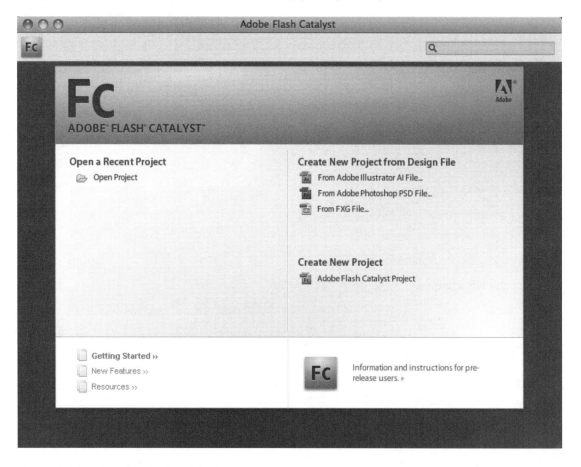

Figure 1-1. Flash Catalyst initial dialog box

The Catalyst Interface

Although Catalyst takes some concepts from the interfaces of other Adobe products such as Flash and Flex, it also has elements that are distinct to it. Figure 1-2 shows the various Catalyst interface elements that you look at in this chapter.

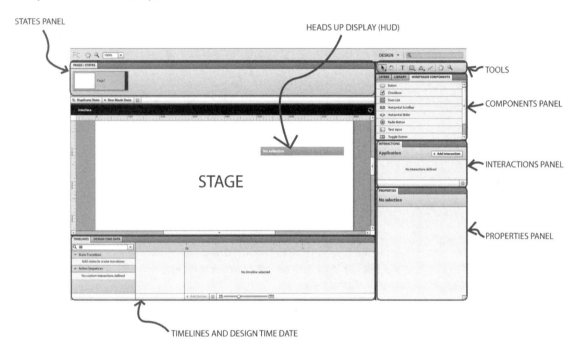

Figure 1-2. Overview of the Catalyst interface

This chapter looks closely at the elements that make up the Flash Catalyst interface and defines the purpose of each panel, to help familiarize you with the interface and related concepts before you dive into the exercises in later chapters.

This section also serves as a reference, so you can come back any time to refresh your memory about the use or definition of any interface element.

Pages/States Panel

Moving clockwise from upper left, you begin at the Pages/States panel. In Catalyst, *pages* and *states* are the same thing. You can think of them as pages if you're used to doing page-based web design. In Flex, these are referred to as *states* (hence the double naming). If you're familiar with Flash, you can also consider them the *keyframes* of your application. Although the terms *states* and *pages* are interchangeable in the context of Catalyst, it's more common to refer to them as states because, in the background, Catalyst is creating Flex states.

States are essentially the different ways your project appears at a given point. For example, if you built a simple web site containing four sections called Home, About, Services, and Contact, they would be your project's states, as shown in Figure 1-3.

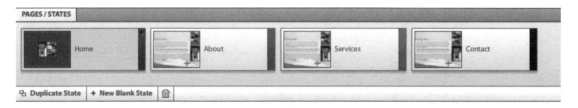

Figure 1-3. Pages/States panel showing a project with four states

At any given point, one of your states is selected. As you place assets onto the stage, they're included in that state and are copied with it if you duplicate the state. You can think of designing in Catalyst as building out a series of pages/states and then moving through them based on user interaction.

By default, Catalyst names the states you create Page1, Page2, and so on, but it's a good idea to name them something that has more meaning in your application (for example, Home, About, Services, and Contact in Figure 1-3). To change the name of a state, double-click the current name in the Pages/States panel, and type in the new name (see Figure 1-4).

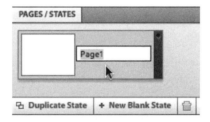

Figure 1-4. Default state name, ready to be changed in the Pages/States panel

Building out your project involves creating new states for each section of your site. You can do this either by creating a new blank state or by duplicating an existing state. To do so, select one of the two options at the bottom of the Pages/States panel (see Figure 1-5).

Figure 1-5. Duplicating the Home state

The majority of the time, you select Duplicate State, because most sites have a variety of shared assets across multiple states (for example, your background image and menu system are likely to stay consistent across all states).

As you create a design, you often have the same assets in different states in different positions or with different properties. For example, a submenu may be visible in one state and hidden in another state. It can become difficult to manage which asset is in which state and in which position, especially as your project grows and you add new assets to later states. To manage this, Catalyst allows you to share or remove individual assets (or groups of assets) across states.

For example, let's say you're creating the four-state project (Home, About, Services, Contact) used as an example previously. As you're building the Contact state, you decide to add a Home button. You realize that you want this button to also exist in the Services state but not in the Home state. You can select the button and use the menus to select States ➤ Share to State ➤ Services, where Services is the name of the state to which you want to share the button (see Figure 1-6). Doing so copies the button to the Services state in the same location and with the same properties as in the Contact state.

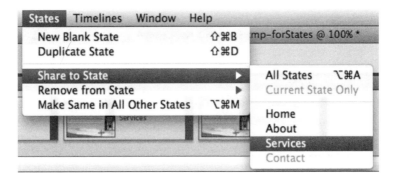

Figure 1-6. Sharing an objects across states

As you can see in the States menu, you can also make an asset the same in all states: that means wherever that asset exists, its properties, position, so forth are the same as for the asset you've selected. This is useful when you move an object in one state but want it to be in the exact same position in the other states. You can also remove an asset from a specific state. In other words, when you select an item, if you decide to copy it or delete it, the asset and all its properties are copied or deleted across all states. You can also access this menu by right-clicking an asset.

Components and States

Catalyst depends heavily on the use of components. *Components* are objects that have a set of reactions based on user interaction. The simplest of these is a button, but components can also be more complicated, such as check boxes and scrollbars. In Catalyst, the reactions of these components are largely set: a scrollbar responds as a scrollbar, and a check box responds as a check box (although you can also create custom components that give you more control over the interaction, as covered in Chapter 9). A set of all the components in Catalyst with a default aesthetic exist in the Wireframe Components panel that you examine later this chapter, but you can also add custom visuals to components. This is where states come back into play.

When you're working with components, Catalyst uses the same idea of states and the same methods to control assets across them. If you drag the simplest component, a button, from the Wireframe Components panel onto the stage and open it by double-clicking it, you find that it has four states, as shown in Figure 1-7: Up, Over, Down, and Disabled. These states give any button its visual appearance based on user interaction. For example, the look of the Up state is seen before the user rolls over the button, the Over state is seen on rollover, and the Down state is seen as the user clicks the button.

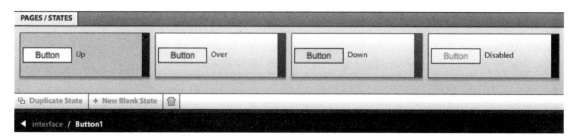

Figure 1-7. Button states

Other components have a similar set of states that define their appearance. You can customize the contents of these states. Because states make up the basis of the project as a whole and the components in it, the techniques, such as animation, that you learn for states can be applied to animating transitions both in the project and in components.

Chapters 2 and 3 look at buttons and other components in greater depth.

Tools

Compared to the tools panels available in other design software such as Photoshop, the Tools panel in Catalyst is pretty bare (see Figure 1-8). This is because most sophisticated graphics work should be done in more specialized programs such as Photoshop, Illustrator, and Fireworks and then brought into Catalyst to make it interactive.

Figure 1-8. Tools panel

You still have the basics available, and they're very useful for creating assets quickly. The Select, Rectangle/Ellipse, and Shape tools have suboptions that you can access by clicking and holding the top option. Let's look at the tools individually:

- Select and Direct Select (Figure 1-9): The Select tool (dark arrow) allows you to select an entire object, whereas the Direct Select tool (light arrow) lets you select individual parts of an object, such as the stroke around a shape.

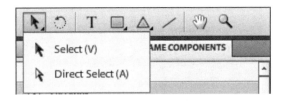

Figure 1-9. Selection tools

- Transform (Figure 1-01): This tool allows you to change an object's scale, rotation, and center point. Scaling allows you to stretch a graphic object by dragging the square handles around it. You can rotate an object by dragging the handles inward with a circular motion. And you can change the center point by dragging the handle displayed in the middle of the object.

Figure 1-10. Transform tool

- Text tool: The Text tool allows you to create point text or area text. Point text is a text object that begins at one point and continues along a single line until the text is complete. Area text is defined by a bounding box created for the text; a new line begins each time the text reaches the edge of the bounding box. To create point text, click the stage with the text tool selected. To create area text, click and drag to create the bounding box (see Figure 1-11). Note that to contain the text in a defined area, it's best to create area text—if you paste text from another document without using area text, the text often overflows the edges of the stage.

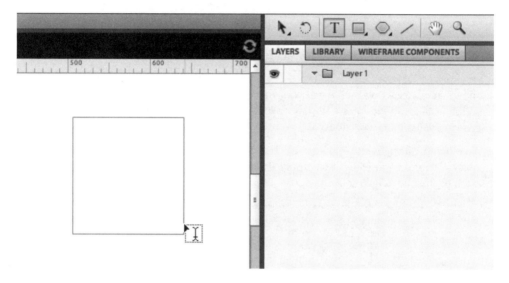

Figure 1-11. Creating area text with the Text tool

- Rectangle/Ellipse (Figure 1-12): To draw using this tool, select the correct variation (for example, Rounded rectangle), and click and drag on the stage. You draw the shape first and then modify its properties (fill color, radius of the corners, and so on) in the Properties panel.

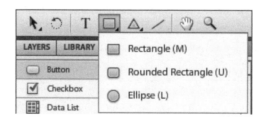

Figure 1-12. Rectangle/Ellipse tool

- Shape (Figure 1-13): This tool provides some basic shapes (triangle, hexagon, octagon, and star), which are useful if you want to quickly create design elements (such as a Play button) or if you get bored and want to starify your entire design.

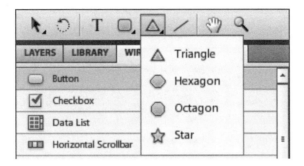

Figure 1-13. Shape tool

- Line: Holding down Shift as you draw with the Line tool restricts the tool to drawing on 90 and 45 degree angles.

- Hand: The Hand tool allows you to move the stage in the software. You can also access this tool by holding down the spacebar.

- Zoom: Select and click the area you want to zoom in on. Hold down Alt (or Option on the Mac) while clicking to zoom out. At upper left in the Catalyst interface, you can see how far you're zoomed in.

The Layers, Library, and Wireframe Components Panels

In Flash Catalyst's default layout, the Layers, Library, and Wireframe Components panels are conveniently grouped together. As you work with projects, you'll interact with these panels all the time, so let's run through them in detail.

Layers

Every asset that is created is given a layer, whether it's created in Catalyst or an outside program. If assets are created externally (in Photoshop or Illustrator), they retain their layer names from the outside program. These layers can quickly become difficult to manage if you don't keep them organized by naming them clearly and grouping multiple layers into sublayers.

You can rearrange layers by using drag and drop in the Layers panel. When an object is created, such as a button or an image, it's automatically given a layer with an image of the object as the layer thumbnail. Any layer or sublayer you create is given a folder icon. These folder layers are used to organize the other object layers. You can drag and drop object layers into the folder layers (with the folder icons) to better organize your project. Figure 1-14, for example, shows the layers containing each menu button placed in a folder layer named Navigation.

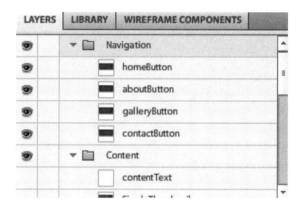

Figure 1-14. Layers and sublayers

The way a layer is shown in the Layers panel also lets you know which object is visible in the current state. Look at Figure 1-15.

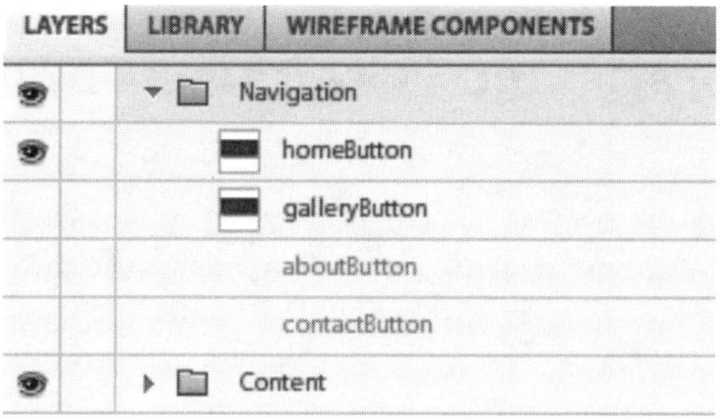

Figure 1-15. Layers panel with layers that are visible, invisible and not present in the state

In Figure 1-15, homeButton exists and is visible in the current state, as indicated by the presence of the eye on that layer. galleryButton exists but isn't visible in this state—it isn't grayed out (meaning it exists), but it also doesn't have an eye icon next to it (meaning it isn't visible). Having layers invisible in a state is useful when you're creating transitions away from the state; Chapter 4 looks at this in detail. aboutButton and contactButton don't exist in this state (they're grayed out), but their presence in the Layers panel indicates that they do exist in another state. As long as an object exists in one of the states, it's listed in the Layers panel; this makes it easier to access objects but can also make for a disorganized project if you don't use folder layers to organize them.

To create a new layer, click the Create New Layer button at the bottom of the Layers panel, as shown in Figure 1-16.

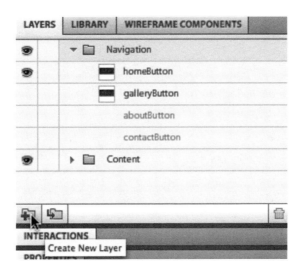

Figure 1-16. Create New Layer button in the Layers panel

Library Panel

The Library panel contains all the components, images, and media that you create in the project. Any components you create based on elements you create in a graphics program are automatically placed in the Library panel. Any images, SWF files, or media files that are imported into the project are also placed in the Library. Figure 1-17 shows the Library panel with four buttons, a set of thumbnail images and a sound clip. If you import a single image, it's placed both on the stage and in the Library, whereas importing a set of images only places them in the Library.

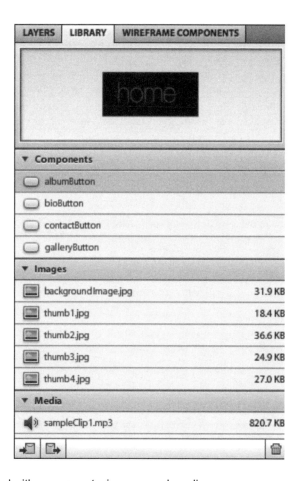

Figure 1-17. Library panel with components, images, and media

The two buttons at lower left in the Library panel allow you to import and export a library package. Library *packages* are a way to share project assets across multiple projects. Chapter 9 looks at this in more detail.

Wireframe Components

Wireframe components have a low-fidelity look. You can use them to quickly create a project that has the interactions and behaviors of the final application without worrying about the visual appearance of the final product. They're also very useful for getting an understanding of the kinds of components you can create in Catalyst. The Wireframe Components panel presents Catalyst's complete set of built-in components (see Figure 1-18). You can create custom components to extend them, as discussed in Chapter 9.

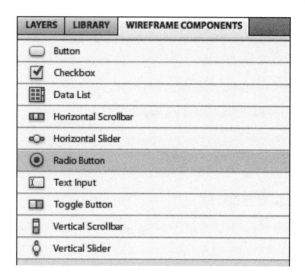

Figure 1-18. The Wireframe Components panel

Wireframes help you create variations of a layout without going into detail on the aesthetics. They're generally used at the start of a project to clarify what is expected in terms of interface and to familiarize all parties involved with the application or web site.

Normally, wireframes are static and don't give a sense of the application's interactions or movement; but with Flash Catalyst, interactions and movement are integrated into the wireframe. This gives you a sense of the user experience much earlier in the process.

As you can see in Figure 1-19, wireframe components have a basic appearance specifically so that when you create a prototype with them, anyone looking at the design knows that they're placeholders and don't represent the final aesthetic of the planned site. It's similar to giving a design a sketch aesthetic before handing it to a client, so they know the design isn't final.

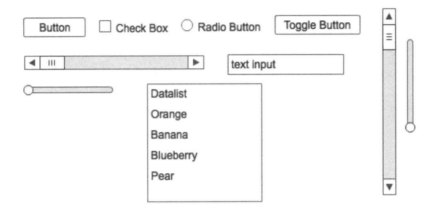

Figure 1-19. Wireframe components placed on the stage

Chapter 3 looks at the use of wireframe components in detail.

The Interactions Panel

The Interactions panel, shown in Figure 1-20, controls what happens in your application based on user interactions. You can place an interaction on any component or on the application itself. To create an interaction, select the component, and click Add Interaction in the Interactions panel. Doing so brings up a set of combo boxes that define the details of the interaction (see Figure 1-21).

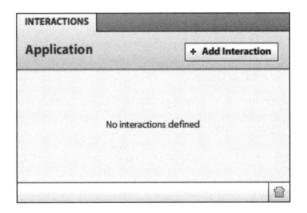

Figure 1-20. Interactions panel before an object is selected

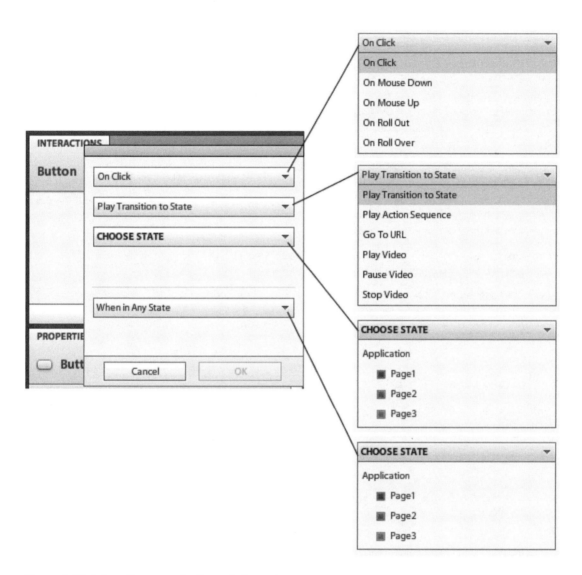

Figure 1-21. Interactions panel with nested panels

The first combo box defines when you want this action to occur—for example, On Click. The second defines what you want to happen; generally, this involves jumping to a different state (Play Transition to State), but you can also choose Play Action Sequence, open a different web page (Go To URL), or control a video file. The Play Action Sequence option lets you trigger an action while staying in the same state. This is useful to trigger action in a SWF file, play a sound, or change the property of a button in the current state. The most common interaction, though, is Play Transition to State, which is why it's the default setting.

If you're playing a transition to a different state, then the third combo box defines which state you're going to. The fourth combo box defines in which state this interaction holds true. Most of the time, the interaction is true in all states—for example, a contact button always does the same thing regardless of the state in which it's clicked. But in some circumstances, it's useful to have objects do different actions depending on the state. An example of this is a Next button.

The Interactions panel changes slightly based on what is selected. For example, a datagrid allows you to define the interaction when any item is selected or when a specific item is selected.

You can also define interactions for the application, in order to trigger actions on the application start. For example, you can have the navigation elements fade in after the application is loaded.

Chapter 5 looks at the Interactions panel in depth.

The Properties Panel

The Properties panel holds a wide variety of settings for each component and object in Catalyst. These settings allow you to define the label on a button, control the opacity of a rectangle, and so on. The properties on the panel affect the appearance of a component including blend modes, filters, and whether the component is enabled.

The Properties panel is context specific, meaning that the properties that are listed changed based on what kind of object is selected. Changes in the Properties panel affect the object in the current state only—this means changing the x position of a button in one state doesn't automatically change it in the other states.

A component's properties are broken into categories. The Common and Component categories, shown in Figure 1-22, include the properties that most components carry, whereas the Appearance category includes the blend modes, the focus ring color, and whether the hand cursor is shown on rollover (see Figure 1-23).

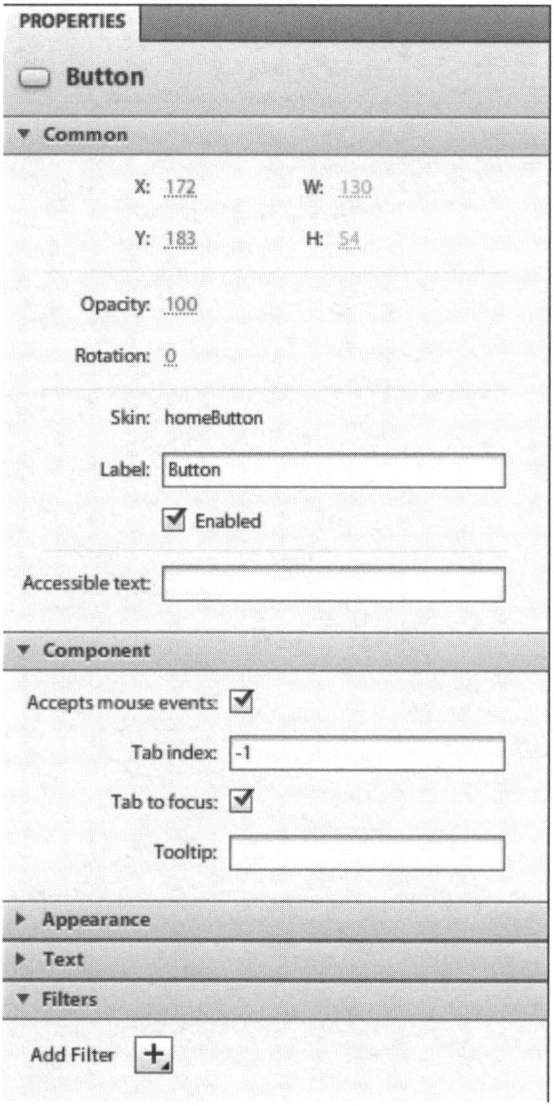

Figure 1-22. Properties panel

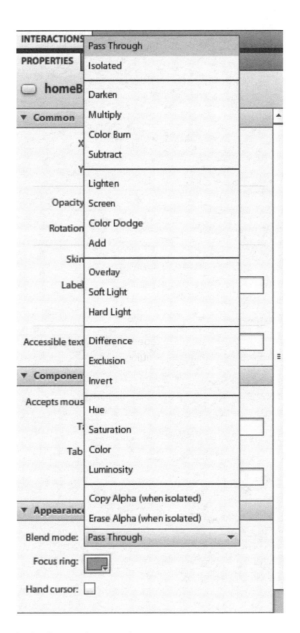

Figure 1-23. Blend modes in the Properties panel

The Text category lets you change the properties of the text in a component, if any (see Figure 1-24).

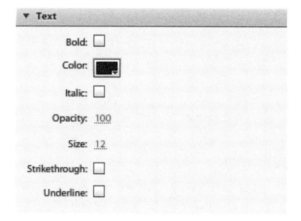

Figure 1-24. Text category in the Properties panel

The final category gives you the object's filter properties (see Figure 1-25). You can apply filters to components, images, and vectors; and you can use multiple filters on a single object.

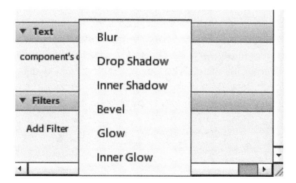

Figure 1-25. Filters

The Timelines Panel

The Timelines panel is the part of the Catalyst interface that controls animation (see Figure 1-26). Although this panel pulls some ideas from Flash timelines and from Flex transitions and effects, working with animations in Catalyst is considerably different.

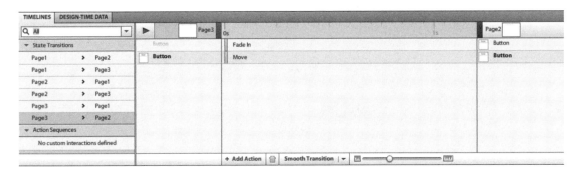

Figure 1-26. Timelines panel

You can create animation in two primary ways in Catalyst: by creating transitions between states and by creating action sequences. Transitions between states are more common, so let's start there.

Catalyst projects are made up of multiple pages/states that change based on user interaction (controlled through the Interactions panel). By default, these changes have no animation associated with them, but you can make the changes smooth by adding timeline transitions. The Timelines panel includes a list of all the possible movements between states. For example, if you have two states, you can move from the first to the second or from the second to the first. As the number of states in your project increases, this list grows exponentially.

Figure 1-27 shows the possible state movements for a Catalyst project that has two states. When one of them is selected, the timeline lists all the components that differ between the two states. Figure 1-28 shows that two buttons are different between the two states. The first button exists only in the first state, so Catalyst sets it to have a Fade Out effect. The second button is in a different position on Page2, so Catalyst sets it to have a Move effect. Both of these transitions currently have a duration of 0 seconds. You can extend this either by pulling them out manually or by clicking the Smooth Transition button.

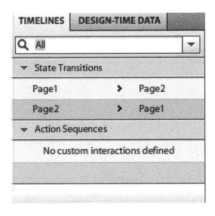

Figure 1-27. The State Transitions list in the Timelines panel

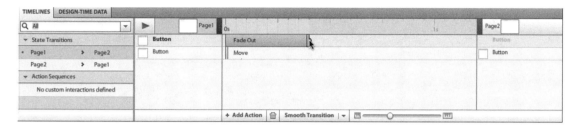

Figure 1-28. Manually extending the duration of a transition

Creating transitions in components (for example, creating a rollover animation for a button) uses the same technique, but it affects the states in the component.

Action sequences are different because they don't involve a change of state. Instead, they can trigger a sound, play a SWF file, or affect a component property while staying in the current state. Changing a component property by using action sequences is done much more rarely that using state transitions, but you can do this to create some unique effects. In Chapter 4, for example, you use action sequences to create a 3D flip effect. Chapter 4 looks closely at animation.

The Design-Time Data Panel

You use the Design-Time Data panel whenever you use a data-list component. Data-list components let you repeat a series of similar objects to create a more complicated object. This comes in very handy when you're creating repeating objects such as thumbnails or menu items. In completed applications, these kinds of elements are often repeated based on live data. The Design-Time Data panel allows you to easily modify the repeated objects so they look similar to live data. Figure 1-29 shows an example of a data-list component.

Creating a data-list component is a multistep process that is shown in detail in Chapter 7; this section just explains it in broad strokes. You first make one instance of the things to be repeated. In the example shown in Figure 1-29, the things to be repeated are an image and two text boxes. When these objects are selected and made into a data list, they're repeated to make a set. Initially, they're all exactly the same. The Design-Time Data panel lets you see the content of each repeated item and easily change an individual item. In Figure 1-29, the second and third images have been changed to make the set look more realistic. The text can also be changed easily to give the impression that it's data being pulled from a database. When the project is handed over to the developer, the design-time data is replaced by live data from a data source.

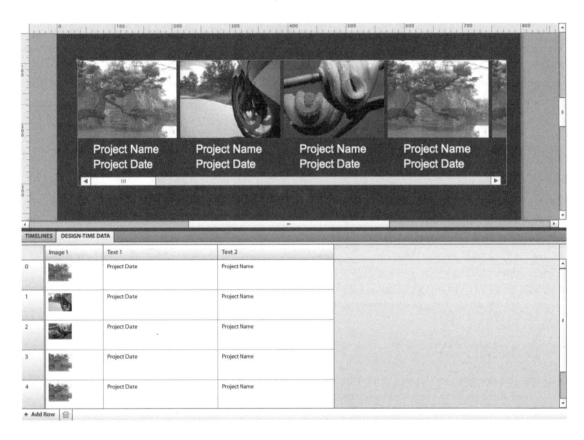

Figure 1-29. Design-Time Data panel

The Stage

Also referred to as the *artboard*, the *stage* is the main area on which you place components. The size and color of the stage are set when you first create your project and define the project's screen size. Unfortunately, it isn't possible to have a fluid layout in a Catalyst project.

The stage provides rulers that can guide your layout, similar to those in Photoshop and Illustrator. Along the top of the stage, a black bar displays Catalyst's breadcrumb navigation, as shown in Figure 1-30.

The breadcrumb navigation lets you know where you are in the project's nesting. In this case, the Catalyst project is named exampleProject, and you're in the button named buttonExample. When you move into a component, the component name is placed in the breadcrumb navigation, and the rest of the design is slightly grayed out. Clicking a part of the breadcrumb navigation takes you to that level in the nesting.

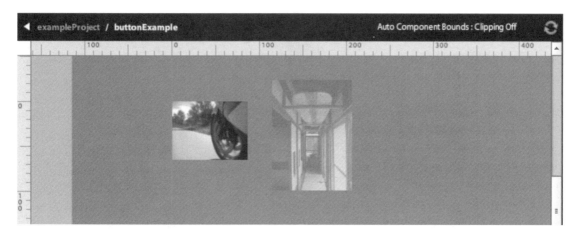

Figure 1-30. The stage showing breadcrumb navigation

Heads-Up Display (HUD)

The final piece of the interface in Catalyst is the Heads-Up Display (HUD). The HUD is unique to Catalyst and gives you context-specific commands related to the object that is currently selected; it essentially tries to guide you through the next logical step of whatever you're currently doing.

For example, if you have an image selected, as in Figure 1-31, the HUD guides you through the next two most likely actions: Convert Artwork to Component and Optimize Artwork.

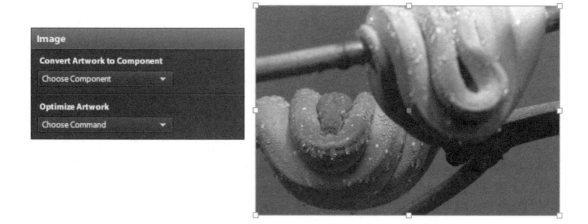

Figure 1-31. Heads-Up Display with an image selected

The HUD is context specific, changing depending on the kind of object selected. Figure 1-32 shows how different the HUD choices are for a button. You'll use the HUD a lot as you work on projects in Flash Catalyst, and you'll find that it significantly increases the speed of your workflow.

Figure 1-32. HUD options for a button

Code View

As you're doing design work, importing graphic elements, changing properties, adding interactions, and smoothing transitions, Catalyst is busy putting your design into a form that a developer can manipulate into the finished project in Flex Builder. You can look at this code by switching to the code view at upper right in the interface. Figure 1-33 shows a very simple application—the code becomes very complex fairly quickly.

```xml
1  <?xml version="1.0" encoding="utf-8"?>
2  <s:Application
3      xmlns:fx="http://ns.adobe.com/mxml/2009" xmlns:s="library://ns.adobe.com/flex/spark"
4      xmlns:d="http://ns.adobe.com/fxg/2008/dt" xmlns:fc="http://ns.adobe.com/flashcatalyst/2009"
5      width="800" height="600" backgroundColor="#FFFFFF" preloaderChromeColor="#FFFFFF">
6      <s:states>
7          <s:State name="Page1"/>
8          <s:State name="Page2"/>
9      </s:states>
10     <fx:DesignLayer d:userLabel="Layer 1">
11         <s:Button label="Home" x="238" y="76" d:userLabel="navButton"/>
12         <s:BitmapImage smooth="true" source="@Embed('/assets/images/0spaceporta.jpg')" x="107" y="103" x.Page2="312" y.Page2="11" id="bit
13     </fx:DesignLayer>
14     <s:transitions>
15         <s:Transition fromState="Page2" toState="Page1" autoReverse="true">
16             <s:Parallel>
17                 <s:Parallel target="{bitmapimage1}">
18                     <s:Move duration="500" autoCenterTransform="true" startDelay="0"/>
19                 </s:Parallel>
20             </s:Parallel>
21         </s:Transition>
22         <s:Transition fromState="Page1" toState="Page2" autoReverse="true">
23             <s:Parallel>
24                 <s:Parallel target="{bitmapimage1}">
25                     <s:Move duration="500" autoCenterTransform="true"/>
26                 </s:Parallel>
27             </s:Parallel>
28         </s:Transition>
29     </s:transitions>
30 </s:Application>
```

Figure 1-33. The code view for a simple application design

Although you can't change any of the code in the code view, it's useful to look at this area as you import assets and build your project to ensure that it stays as neat as possible for the developer. You do this primarily by using a consistent, clear naming convention for all your components. Naming conventions and other best practices are covered in Chapter 6.

Conclusion

Now that you've had a look around and gotten an initial impression of the tools available to you in Catalyst, you're ready to dive into creating your first project. Whereas this chapter was meant to familiarize you with interface, the next chapter shows you how to move from Illustrator assets into a full interactive animated project. It shows how the various aspects of Catalyst come together to rapidly create a fully functioning prototype. The chapters that follow it drill deeper into specific aspects of Catalyst.

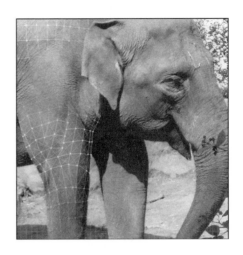

Chapter 2

Your First Flash Catalyst Project

What we'll cover in this chapter:

- Bringing in a site design from Photoshop

- Converting Photoshop assets to buttons

- Simple animation in Catalyst

- Simple interactions in Catalyst

Files used in this chapter:

- musicSiteDesign.psd

- BioAndAlbum.txt

- sampleClip.mp3

- thumb1.jpg, thumb2.jpg, and thumb3.jpg

Flash Catalyst is designed to let you take assets created in Photoshop or Illustrator and convert them into an interactive prototype of the final site. It allows you, for example, to take a static image and essentially tell it to act like a button. You can then control when parts of your design are visible and how they're made visible. Catalyst gives you a very quick way to move from static images in a graphics program to an interactive dynamic project.

In this chapter's first example, you create a simple promotional web site for the talented Toronto musician Amanda Moscar (`http://AmandaMoscar.com`). You can see the final site at `http://greggoralski.com/amandamoscar`. The visual assets for the site have been created for you in a Photoshop file. You use these graphics, bringing them into Catalyst and giving them the behaviors and transitions of the site. Let's get started by looking over the Photoshop file, shown in Figure 2.1.

Figure 2-1. Photoshop assets for the example project

This Photoshop file contains a variety of layers that contain a background; a logo; three different images of Amanda to form the background of the web site's three sections; some text; and the Up, Down, and Over states of a Play button (contained in the `playButton` folder). In the example, the logo stays consistent in all of the site's states, whereas the background image changes depending on which section of the site you're on. The text forms some of the content for each section; and the Up, Down, and Over states in the `playButton` folder create a single button that plays a sample of Amanda's music.

Figure 2-2 shows the structure of the Photoshop layers.

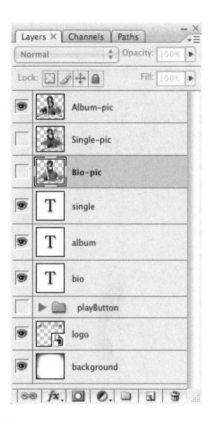

Figure 2-2. Naming of layers in Photoshop

Creating a Catalyst Project from a Photoshop PSD File

To create the site, begin by opening Flash Catalyst. The Catalyst welcome screen of (Figure 2-3) gives you three main options: to open an existing Catalyst project, to create a new project from a design file, or to create a new project directly in Catalyst. The third option is useful when you want to begin a project based on a sketch, as you see in this chapter. For this project, you create the project from a design file. You can create your Catalyst project from a Photoshop file, an Illustrator file, or an FXG (Flash XML graphics—this format is covered in Chapter 6).

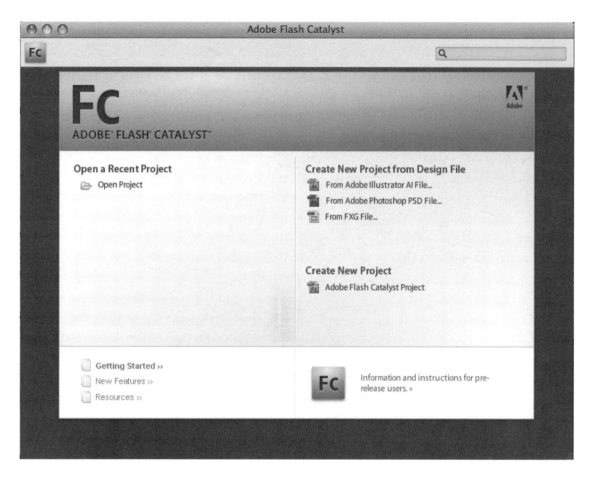

Figure 2-3. Flash Catalyst welcom screen

Follow these steps:

1. Select the From Adobe Photoshop PSD File option, and then select the musicSiteDesign.psd file. The Photoshop Import Options dialog box automatically sets your project's width and height to match your Photoshop file's artboard. You can stick with the default settings at this stage, although you may want to change the background color to something more consistent with the design, as shown in Figure 2-4. The background color defines the background of the stage in Catalyst and also the color of the HTML file that contains the project when viewed in a browser.

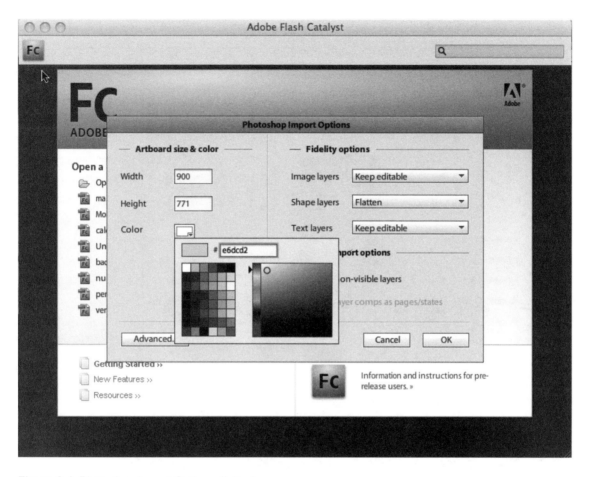

Figure 2-4. Photoshop Import Options dialog box

2. Click OK to close the Import Options dialog box. The design now opens in Catalyst.

3. Select the Layers panel. Note that all of your layers from Photoshop, including those that weren't visible, are available for you to work with (see Figure 2-5).

Figure 2-5. Photoshop assets imported into Catalyst

Converting Photoshop Artwork into a Button

From your Photoshop file, you have three pieces of static text to serve as your menu of buttons (Bio, Album, and Single). A button is a good place to look at how Catalyst takes static graphic elements and makes them dynamic and interactive. By converting artwork—in this case, a word—into a button component, you give that artwork the behavior of a button. This means it can have a different appearance depending on user interactions, and it can trigger other actions. The way the button looks depends on whether the user has rolled over or clicked the button, and this is controlled by the button's Over and Down states, respectively. The actions associated with the user clicking or rolling over the button are controlled via the Interactions panel; you create interactions for a button later this chapter.

Follow these steps to turn the word *bio* into a button:

1. Select the *bio* text by clicking it on the screen or in the Layers panel. Selecting the text brings up the Heads-Up Display (HUD) floating panel (see Figure 2-6).

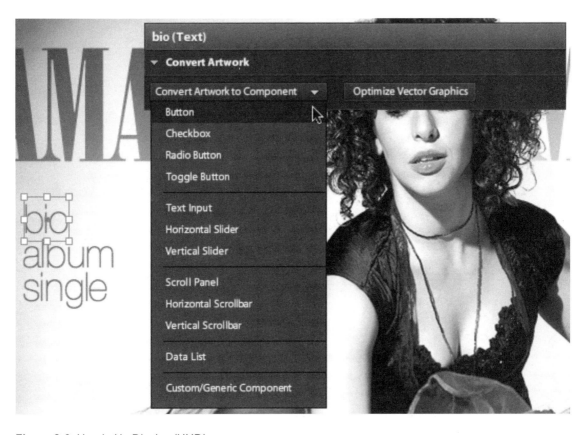

Figure 2-6. Heads-Up Display (HUD)

2. In this case, you want to convert the piece of text into a component, specifically a button component. Select Convert Artwork ➤ Convert Artwork to Component ➤ Button from the combo box, as shown in Figure 2-6. The HUD changes to guide you through the next stage: defining the way the button looks in its Up, Over, Down, and Disabled states.

3. Select Edit Button Appearance ➤ Over in the HUD (see Figure 2-7). The button states appear in the States panel at the top of the screen. Selecting the text shows its properties in the Properties panel.

Figure 2-7. Accessing button states via the HUD

4. In the Properties panel, change the text to the color you want it to be when the user rolls over it. Burgundy works well here (see Figure 2-8).

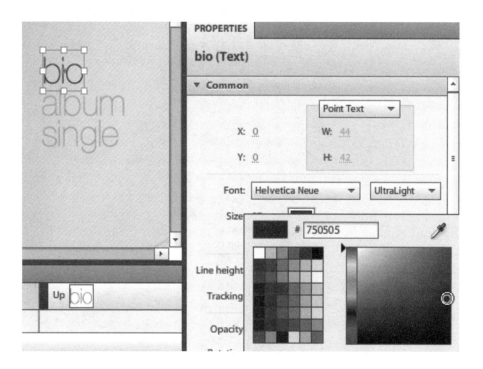

Figure 2-8. Changing the text's color in the Properties panel

5. Select the button's Down state in the States panel, and change the text's color to a brighter red. You can ignore the Disabled state, because you don't disable this button in this design.

6. While you're changing the button's states, you're inside the button. A button's states work similarly to the main project's states, but they're nested in the button. To jump back to the main stage, you can use the breadcrumb navigation elements directly below the States panel: click musicSiteDesign, as shown in Figure 2-9.

Figure 2-9. Breadcrumb navigation

7. Test your design to see the button in action: choose File ➤ Run Project (see Figure 2-10).

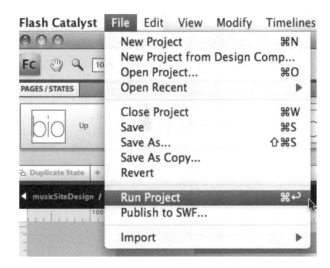

Figure 2-10. Running the project via the main menu

8. When you're satisfied with your color choices, repeat steps 1–5 for the Album and Single buttons.

Presenting Content

Next, you need to create an area for the presentation of the content. The content that has been provided is text for the Bio, Album, and Single areas (BioAndAlbum.txt), a song (sampleClip.mp3), and three thumbnail images to use in the design (thumb1.jpg, thumb2.jpg, and thumb3.jpg). To present the content on top of the background images without losing the effect of the images, you create a partially transparent rectangle to define the content area. This is also an example of how you can create simple graphic elements in Catalyst.

Follow these steps:

1. From the Tools panel, select the Rectangle tool. Draw a rectangle to define the area you want to use for your content, as shown in Figure 2-11. To change this from a white box to something more consistent with the design, you can change its properties.

Figure 2-11. Creating a content area in the design

2. In the Properties panel, change the stroke and fill. To select colors that are consistent with the design, use the Eye Dropper tool in the color selector (see Figure 2-12) to select a color sample from the stage.

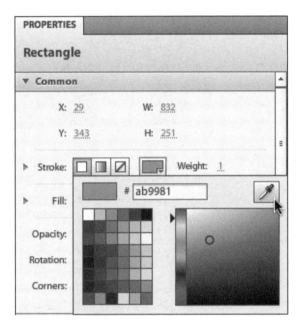

Figure 2-12. Color selector in the rectangle's Properties panel

3. In the Properties panel, change the rectangle's Opacity to 90% (allowing some of the image to show through), and round the corners (10px). As a small additional touch, you can also add a drop shadow in the Filters section of the Properties panel. The resulting rectangle should look as it does in Figure 2-13; it's considerably more at home in the design.

4. To add the text, open `BioAndAlbum.txt` in a simple text editor (such as Notepad or TextEdit), and copy the bio paragraph. Back in Catalyst, use the Text tool from the Tools panel to create a text area for the text (by clicking and dragging).

5. Click into the text box you just created, and paste the text into it. Again, you need to use the Properties panel to make the design consistent (see Figure 2-14). Helvetica Neue Light at 15 pt works well.

Figure 2-13. Content area with partial transparency and a drop shadow

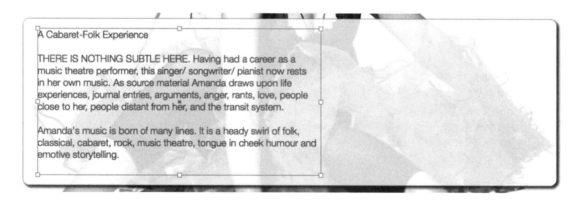

Figure 2-14. Text box added to the content area

6. Import the thumbnail image for this section (`thumb1.jpg`) by selecting File ➤ Import ➤ Image, as shown in Figure 2-15. Doing so brings the image into the project. Similar to the text box, you can alter the image using the Properties panel.

Figure 2-15. Importing an images via the main menu

7. Move the thumbnail image onto the content area, and add a drop shadow through the Properties panel.

8. To keep your project organized, in the Layers panel, rename the text area **BioText**, the thumbnail **BioThumbnail**, and the rectangle **ContentArea** (see Figure 2-16).

You've now created the appearance you want for your design's Bio state, but you haven't created the new state for it (all your work so far has been in the Page1 state that was automatically created). You have two options for how to proceed with creating the content for subsequent states: you can create a new state and add the content in it, or you can place all the content in one state and then copy that state (making different parts of the content visible in each state). The first technique has the advantage of taking a bit less processing power (because there is less duplication of the content), whereas the second technique gives you more options for animations (such as sliding in from the side). Because in this case you're more concerned with animation than processing, you use the second technique.

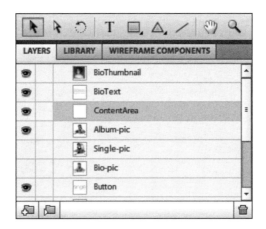

Figure 2-16. Layers panel with the ContentArea rectangle selected

9. Make the BioText and BioThumbnail layers invisible by clicking the eye icon associated with them, as shown in Figure 2-17.

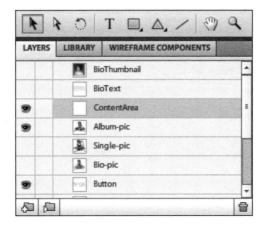

Figure 2-17. Layers panel with the BioThumbnail and BioText layers made invisible

10. Repeat steps 4–8 using the Album text from the `BioAndAlbum.txt` and the thumbnail from `thumb2.jpg` (see Figure 2-18).

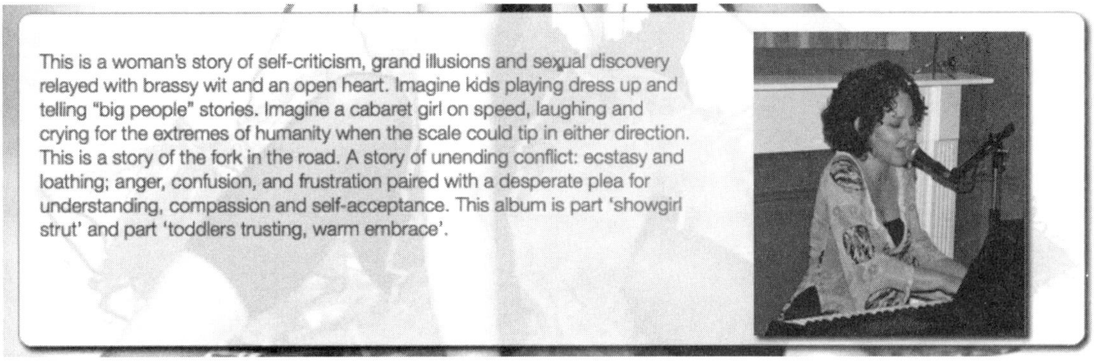

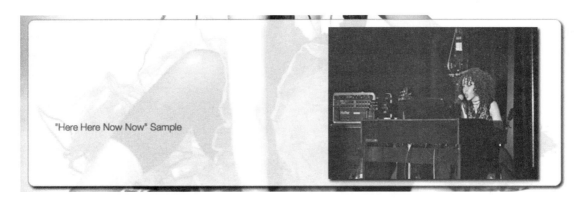

Figure 2-18. Content area with album information and an image

11. Repeat steps 4–8 using the Single text from `BioAndAlbum.txt` and `thumb3.jpg` (see Figure 2-19). The Single section also has a Play button, which you build later in this chapter.

Figure 2-19. Content area with a sample song and an image

Organizing into States

You've created the content for the site, but it's all contained in one state. States, as mentioned in Chapter 1, are the main organizational structure for the sections of your site. They're the pages of the site that the user moves through based on their interactions. In this example, and in most projects, the user's primary interaction is to transition to a different state.

The technique you use in this design has all the content exist in each state—but each piece of content is visible only in the appropriate state. It's also possible for some content not to exist in a state, if you delete it instead of making it invisible; but to keep this example easy to understand, you make the content invisible (as you did in the previous section). This approach also makes it easier to create transitions with movement, as you see.

The first state is your initial page and shows just the background and menu. Follow these steps:

1. Make all the layers invisible except for menu and background elements (the result looks like Figure 2-20). To make a layer invisible, click the eye icon for that layer so the eye disappears.

Figure 2-20. Layout with content area–related layers made invisible

2. Click Duplicate State in the Pages/States panel. Doing so creates a copy of the initial state.

3. Rename the copy **Bio** by double-clicking its name in the Pages/States panel, as shown in Figure 2-21. Also rename the first state **Home**. It's good practice to give your states clear, consistent names so they're easier to organize. (It's also much easier for the developer, who works with the code that Catalyst creates, to understand how to work with a state named Home rather than Page1.

Figure 2-21. Duplicating and naming a state

4. In the newly created state, make the layers to be displayed in the Bio section visible by clicking each layer so the eye icon appears. These layers include BioText, BioThumbnail, ContentArea, and Bio-Pic. The resulting design should look like Figure 2-22.

Figure 2-22. Layout with the bio information and images visible

You've now created the appearance of the Bio state/page. You can follow a similar process to create the other states/pages needed for this project Album and Single, which correspond to the two other buttons on the main menu. For each of these, you need to create the new state, name the state, and then select the layers that should be visible in each state.

5. Repeat steps 2–4 for the Album state, making the AlbumText, AlbumThumbnail, ContentArea, and Album-Pic layers visible. The resulting state is shown in Figure 2-23.

Figure 2-23. Layout with the album information and images visible

6. Repeat steps 2–4 for the Single state, making the SingleText, SingleThumbnail, ContentArea, and Single-Pic layers visible. The resulting state is shown in Figure 2-24.

Figure 2-24. Layout with single information and images visible

With this, you've created the project's main states, which are the way that the site will look like at various times. Which state is seen at which time is controlled by the interactions you place on the menu buttons. Let's look at that now.

Building Interactivity

You need to give your buttons the ability to move the user to different states. You do so using the Interactions panel. This panel lets you add a variety of different kinds of interactions to components. The simplest and most common interaction, which you create in this example, makes a button transition to a specific state when clicked. (The Interactions panel is covered in more detail in Chapter 5.)

Let's start with the Bio button. When the user clicks the Bio button, you want the state to change to the Bio state, showing the appropriate content for that button. (Note that when you add an interaction to a button, it doesn't matter which state you add it to—the interaction goes with the button regardless of state.) Follow these steps:

1. Select the Bio button. In the Interactions panel, select Add Interaction. Doing so opens a menu of options for this button's interactions (see Figure 2-25): what you want to happen, such as a state change; and when you want it to happen (generally on a click or rollover).

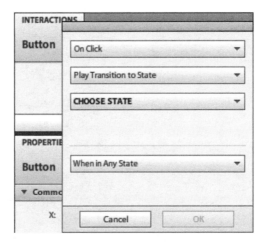

Figure 2-25. Interactions panel

2. Leaving all the other options set to the defaults, select Bio from the Choose State pull-down.

3. Do the same for the Album button, but select Album from the Choose State pull-down.

4. Do the same for the Single button, but select Single from the Choose State pull-down.

5. Test the project by selecting File ➤ Run Project.

The site's buttons now let the user jump to the project's various pages/states.

Adding Animation

One of the key advantages of Catalyst over static comps is the ability to include animation in your prototype. Because animation and feedback are important aspects of interaction design, having control over these aspects from the beginning can lead to better interfaces. Animation is an important feature of Catalyst, and Chapter 4 discusses it in greater detail.

Creating animation in Catalyst is remarkably simple using the Timelines panel. First, let's try the one-click method:

1. Expand the space given to the Timelines panel so you can see all the state transitions by dragging along the top of the panel, as shown in Figure 2-26. At left are all the possible transitions between the project's states; as the number of states in a project increases, this list grows exponentially. Initially, the Home ➤ Bio state transition is selected. Along the timeline are all the design elements that differ between the two states.

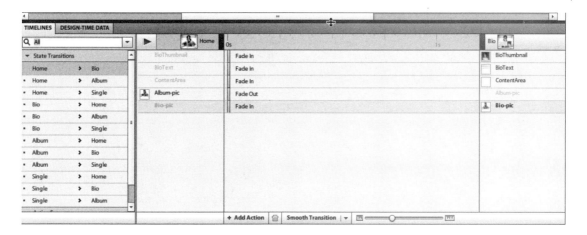

Figure 2-26. Timelines panel

2. Click the Smooth Transition button, as shown in Figure 2-27.

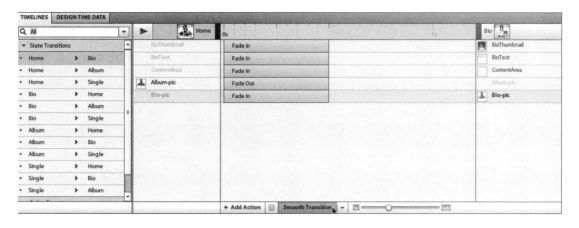

Figure 2-27. Timelines panel with Smooth Transitions

With that single click, the transition Home ➤ Bio now has a variety of fades for the elements that differ between the two states. You can see this in action by running the project and clicking Bio. The default is a half-second transition with a default easing effect. *Easing* controls the speed of the transition, slowing it at the beginning and end to create a more natural effect. Chapter 4 explores different kinds of easing.

Because all your elements are either visible or invisible in a given page/state, the transition that is created is a *fade*. If the elements were in a different location, the transition would automatically change to a *move*; and if the elements were of different sizes, the transition would be a *scale*.

Again, With More Control

Because default settings always end up looking like defaults, you need greater control over the transitions. To the right of Smooth Transitions is a button that opens the transition settings (see Figure 2-28).

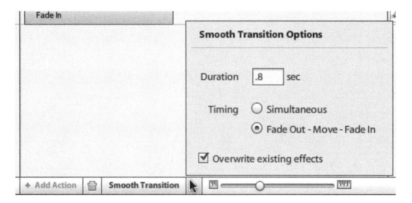

Figure 2-28. Smooth Transition options

Using these settings, you can alter the duration of a transition and change transitions from being simultaneous to a setting called Fade Out - Move - Fade In. You can think of Simultaneous as a crossfade, with all the changes happening at once. The Fade Out - Move - Fade In setting removes the elements from the starting state before bringing in the elements from the ending state; this creates a more complicated transition, with the elements from the first state fading out before the elements from the second state fade in.

Enter a transition duration of **0.8** seconds, select the Fade Out - Move - Fade In setting, and select Overwrite Existing Effects. In order to have a similar transition for all the pages/states, highlight all the transitions by selecting the first transition, holding Shift, and selecting the last transition. Click Smooth Transition. Doing so changes the global settings for Smooth Transition and applies them to all the possible state transitions, as shown in Figure 2-29.

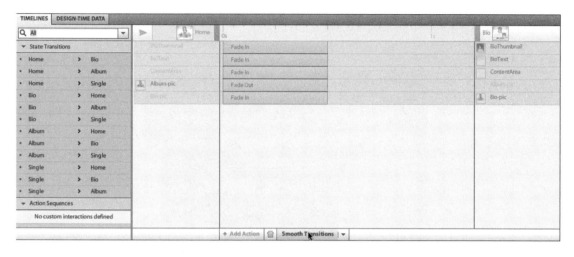

Figure 2-29. Smooth Transitions applied to all state transitions

Choose File ➤ Run Project to see the transitions in action.

Creating Buttons with Transitions

Transitions aren't used exclusively for changes in pages/states. Often, they're even more important for giving users feedback about individual components. To explore this, in this section you create a Play button for the sample song, with a rollover effect for the button. Follow these steps:

1. Select the Single page/state in the Pages/States panel.

2. The visual representation of this button was created in the original Photoshop file in the `playButton` folder. In the Layers panel, open the `playButton` folder to reveal the three layers that make up this button: one for the Up state, one for the Over state, and one for the Down State, as shown in Figure 2-30.

Figure 2-30. Layers of `playButton`

3. Make sure the `playButton` folder is visible, and then select all the layers in the folder.

4.   In the HUD, select Convert Artwork to Component ➤ Choose Component ➤ Button, as shown in Figure 2-31.

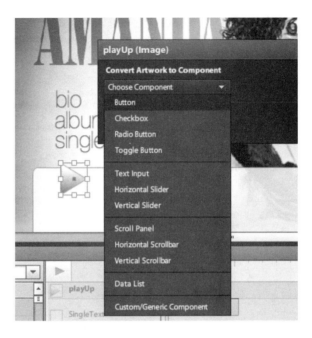

Figure 2-31. Selecting Button from the HUD

5.   Now that the layers have been converted into buttons, you need to make the correct layer visible in each state. In the HUD, select Edit Button Appearance ➤ Up (see Figure 2-32).

Figure 2-32. Accessing button states via the HUD

6.   For each button state, make only the appropriate layer visible by setting the eye icon on its layer: for the Up state, make only playUp visible; for the Over state, make only playOver visible; and for the Down state, make only playDown visible. Ignore the Disabled state, because you aren't using that functionality in this example. The resulting states appear as shown in Figure 2-33.

Figure 2-33. States of the Play button

7. Just like changes in states made on the main stage, changes in button states also have a Timelines panel section for transitions (see Figure 2-34). In the Timelines panel, select all the state transitions (at left), and click Smooth Transitions; the result is shown in Figure 2-35.

Figure 2-34. Timelines panel for the Play button

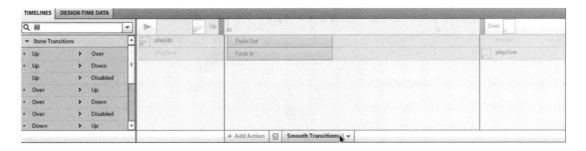

Figure 2-35. Timelines panel with Smooth Transitions applied

You can now position the button on the stage. Testing the movie by choosing File ➤ Run Project shows that the button does a slow fade across its states as the user rolls over and clicks it.

Playing Sound

Now that you've created the Play button, you can add an interaction to play the sound clip that is provided with the files for this chapter (sampleClip.mp3). Playing a sound is an interesting interaction in Catalyst and allows you to look at the other primary option in the Interactions panel: Play Action Sequence.

In order to play a sound, you must first import it, much the same way that you import an image. Import sampleClip.mp3 by choosing File ➤ Import ➤ Video/Sound File (see Figure 2-36). The sound file is placed in the Library in a category called Media (see Figure 2-37).

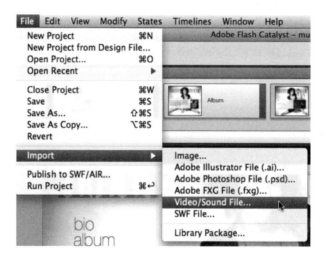

Figure 2-36. Importing a sound file

Figure 2-37. Sound file in the Library

Playing a sound involves creating an action sequence for the interaction and then including Play Sound in that action sequence. An *action sequence* in Catalyst is a set of actions that are triggered but don't involve a state change. In this case, the process starts in the Interactions panel for `playButton`:

1. Select `playButton` on the stage, and, in the Interactions panel, select Add Interaction.

2. Set the interaction to be On Click ➤ Play Action Sequence, as shown in Figure 2-38, and click OK. Doing so creates an action sequence for this event. Action sequences are located just below the transitions in the Timelines panel, as shown in Figure 2-39.

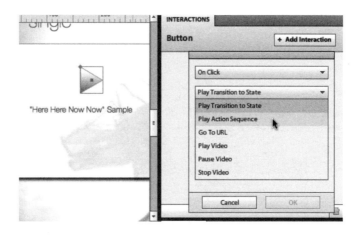

Figure 2-38. Play Action Sequence setting in the Interactions panel

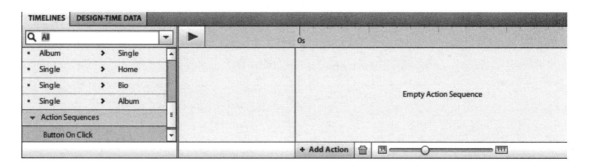

Figure 2-39. Action sequence for the Play button in the Timelines panel

3. You can add a variety of actions to an action sequence, including controlling a SWF, changing the properties of a component, controlling a video, or, in this case, playing a sound. With the action sequence selected, click Add Action, and select Sound Effect (see Figure 2-40). Doing so opens a dialog box where you can choose the sound file you wish to play.

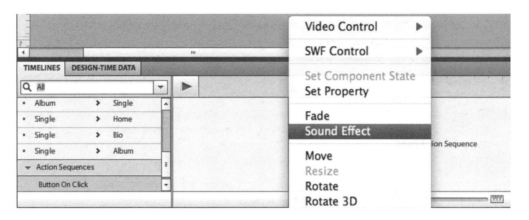

Figure 2-40. Choosing the Sound Effect action

4. Select the sound file sampleClip.mp3, and click OK (see Figure 2-41). Doing so places the sound file in the action sequence and adds it to the timeline, as shown in Figure 2-42.

Figure 2-41. Selecting a sound file

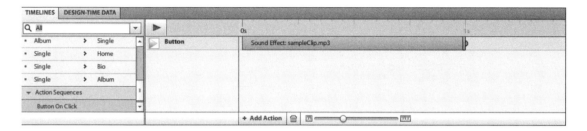

Figure 2-42. The sound file added to the action sequence

5. By default, the sound file is given a one-second duration. Because this sound clip is longer (51 seconds, to be exact), you need to give it more time on the timeline. You can do this by setting the duration of the sound to 51 seconds in the Properties panel , as shown in Figure 2-43.

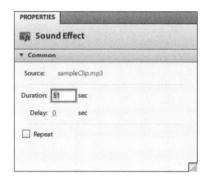

Figure 2-43. Changing the sound file's duraction

Test your Catalyst file, and try the Play button. The audio should begin playing when you click the button.

Conclusion

You've now created your first Catalyst project, taking a static design from a Photoshop file and creating an interactive prototype that could be shown to a client.

In this chapter, you've worked with some of Catalyst's core functionality. You walked through how to convert static Photoshop artwork into components (in the form of the menu buttons and the Play button) and how to use those components to control the states of an application. You also learned how to create the states of a project and transition across them.

This chapter's example is based on a production process that creates the design first in Photoshop and then makes it interactive/animated in Catalyst. The next chapter looks at how to use Catalyst to create interactive wireframes from scratch rather than basing them on an existing design.

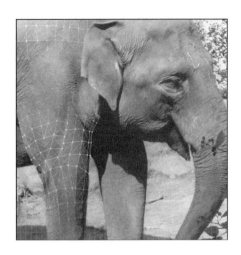

Chapter 3

Wireframing in Catalyst

What we'll cover in this chapter:

- Sketching in the context of Catalyst

- Using the wireframe components

- Using the Data List component

Files used in this Chapter:

- `wireframeComplete.fxp`

Chapter 2 looked at how to use a Photoshop file to create an interactive prototype complete with animations. Another major use of Catalyst is the creation of wireframes. In the context of Flash Catalyst, *wireframing* is the use of simplified, low-fidelity components to quickly sketch out the site and its interaction.

Before you begin building a wireframe in Catalyst, this chapter first talks a bit about sketching and its key characteristics as they apply to Catalyst.

Sketching, Wireframing, and Prototyping Interactivity

The process of sketching, wireframing, and prototyping is often misunderstood. More often than not, designers confuse the meaning of these terms and their importance in the design and development process.

In the design process, sketching is a way to quickly get ideas down on paper (or screen) and communicate them to other members of the design team. Sketches are quick, cheap, plentiful, and disposable. They're meant to suggest and explore ideas as opposed to being complete designs. They're low fidelity out of necessity (because it would take longer to create properly branded, visually stunning components), but the low fidelity also serves the purpose of communicating that this is one design idea, not the final design idea.

The most common form of sketch, and the one that unifies most design fields, is the paper sketch. Nothing is as quick, cheap, or disposable as a sketch put down on paper (see Figure 3-1). And this form of sketch is an important part of any design process (many a great idea/company was first sketched out on a napkin). But there are some limitations of paper sketches as they apply to interaction design. This is partly due to the importance of motion in interaction design. It matters for the user experience how something moves and reacts to the user. Catalyst tries to cover this limitation by allowing you to create a digital sketch that has the same characteristics as a paper sketch—quick, cheap, plentiful, and disposable—while also including movement and behavior in the sketch. (A detailed look at the power of sketching in interaction is available in Bill Buxton's book *Sketching User Experiences.*)

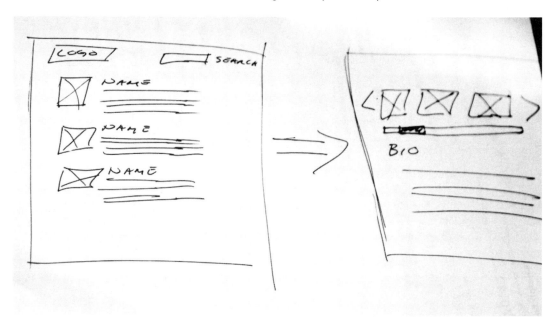

Figure 3-1. Paper sketch

As you move through the creation of your first wireframe, keep in mind these characteristics of sketches to see the stages of the design process in which they apply. The wireframing process is a bit different. Wireframing is more about exploring and further refining the concepts that are born out of sketching and also better communicating those concepts to a team.

In a way, Catalyst brings the two processes together. You use wireframe components to quickly sketch out the interaction and movement of an application. The resulting sketch can then also be solidified into a wireframe that is used to define the specifications of the application.

The line dividing sketching, wireframing, and prototyping is faint, and Flash Catalyst makes it even more difficult to separate one from the other. It's important for the designer or developer to manually enforce these stages in the conceptualization of a project.

Whenever possible, take the time to explore interactions, because they add value to the final product. Sometimes, the details that make an application or interface stand out from the rest are discovered in this process.

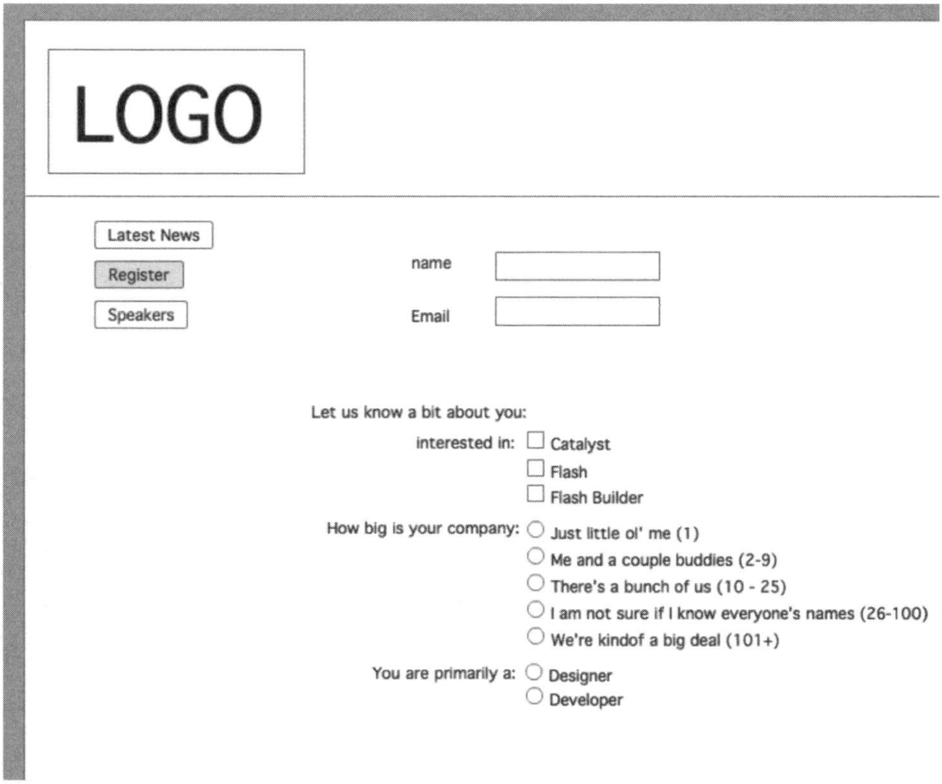

Figure 3-2. Wireframe

Starting the Project

This chapter explores wireframing and prototyping a simple conference site. You create wireframes for the different pages that make up the site. The chapter focuses on creating interactive wireframes rather than visual design. You also become more familiar with the diversity of prebuilt components in Catalyst, because the wireframe components are merely low-fidelity versions of the full components that are available. After you've completed this chapter, you'll understand how to harness the wireframing and prototyping capabilities of Adobe Flash Catalyst to use them in your own projects.

Let's begin by creating a new Catalyst file. In the example in Chapter 2, you created a project based on a Photoshop file that already included the visuals for your project. Here, you start with a blank slate; and sketch a design for a Catalyst conference primarily using the drawing tools and wireframe components contained in Catalyst. Follow these steps:

1. Select Create New Project ➤ Adobe Flash Catalyst Project from the initial dialog box shown in Figure 3-3, and name the project **Catalyst Conference**. You can leave the default settings for Artboard Size and Color.

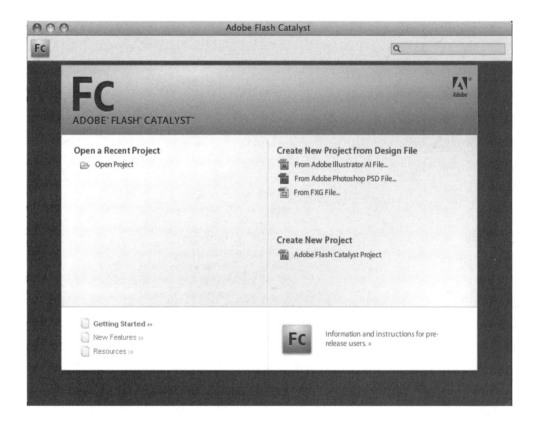

Figure 3-3. Initial Catalyst dialog box

2. You begin with a blank document. Along the top, the default page/state is named Page1. To make it a bit clearer, double-click Page1, and rename it **latestNews** (see Figure 3-4). This is the first page of your application, which shows the latest news regarding the conference.

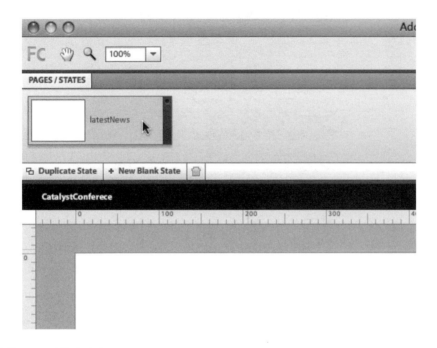

Figure 3-4. Renamed first state

3. At upper right in the interface are Catalyst's drawing tools. In a sketch, you can use the drawing tools to define specific areas and the layout of the overall design. Use the Rectangle drawing tool to specify the area that will ultimately be occupied by the logo in the design, as shown in Figure 3-5.

The default settings for a rectangle in Catalyst are white fill with a 1 px blue stroke. It's a good idea to maintain this default setting for your drawn elements because it's consistent with the visual style of the wireframe components and it reinforces the idea that color isn't an important part of the sketch. Instead, you want anyone who looks at this sketch to give feedback about the sections, movement, and interactions. The visual design and branding should come further down the design process.

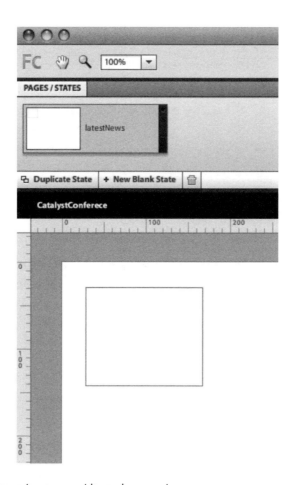

Figure 3-5. Rectangle drawn to represent logo placement

4. To make it clear what this section is for, use the text tool to write the word **LOGO** inside the rectangle. Using the Properties panel, change the font size of the word to better match the rectangle, as shown in Figure 3-6.

Figure 3-6. Text representing the logo

In Chapter 2, you looked at how to create a button based on art that was previously created in Photoshop. But in a wireframe, you're specifically trying not to focus attention on the visual design of the components. Instead, you're trying to keep attention focused on the structure and behavior of the wireframe. For this reason, you want to use generic-looking components. Catalyst provides a set of components with a generic look in the Wireframe Components panel, directly below the Tools panel at upper right in the interface (see Figure 3-7).

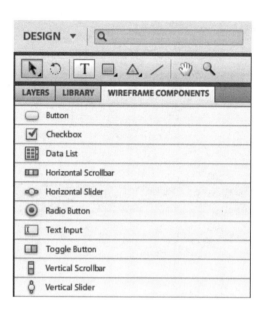

Figure 3-7. Wireframe Components panel

Let's continue building out this first page design, starting with the menu. You saw a basic button in Chapter 2, so let's use a slightly more sophisticated button here. In this example, you use a toggle button to create the main menu.

    5.   Drag an instance of the Toggle Button component from the Wireframe Components panel onto the stage, placing it below the logo as shown in Figure 3-8.

Figure 3-8. Toggle button placement

A toggle button is similar to a regular button except that it has a different look when it's selected. You can test this by running the project as it's set up so far (File ➤ Run Project): the button has a blue-tinted selected state. This reinforces for the user which section they're currently on. To take a closer look at the structure of the toggle button, double-click the button to enter it.

Inside, you can see the states that are available for a toggle button. There are the same states you saw in a regular button (Up, Over, Down, and Disabled) and an additional set representing the button in its selected state (Selected, Up; Selected, Over; Selected, Down; and Selected, Disabled). Figure 3-9 shows the look of the toggle button in each of its states. If you're creating a toggle button from artwork, you can modify each state. Radio buttons and check boxes share this same state structure.

Figure 3-9. Appearance of a wireframe toggle button in each of its states

Let's look at the toggle button's properties. You can find the Properties panel at right in the interface below the Interactions panel. Because you're trying to stick with a generic look for your components, the only properties you want to change are Label and Selected (see Figure 3-10).

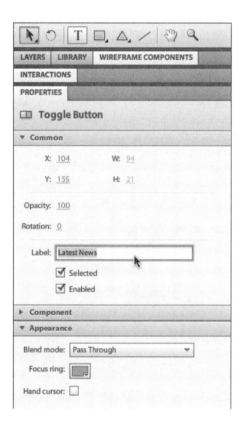

Figure 3-10. Toggle button properties

6. For the toggle button, set the Label property to **Latest News**. Select the Selected check box, to make this toggle button selected on this page/state. By having the button for each state selected, you create the look of a highlighted menu item for that page.

This wireframe has two more sections: Register (in which you use the wireframe components to create a page to elicit info from the user) and Speakers (in which you use the Data List component to create a layout for speaker information). Each section needs a toggle button.

7. Create two more toggle buttons below the first one. Set their labels to **Register** and **Speakers**. Don't select the Selected check box for either. The result should look like Figure 3-11.

Figure 3-11. Toggle buttons in position

8. In the first state/page, you define the layout for a simple news page. Essentially, each news item consists of an image, a title, and the body text. To keep things simple, and to reinforce that speed is important for wireframing, in this example you create these by using the drawing and text tools in Catalyst's Tools panel. Create the image area by drawing a rectangle with two lines though it. Create a text area by using the Text tool: click and drag to define the size of the text area. Fill the text area with Loren Ipsum text (you can generate some at www.lipsum.com). You can also create the title using the Text tool, but we've just left a single text box that will include the title and body text. There is no need to tinker with the fonts, because the emphasis is on speed and a generic look. Create a line along the top to define the edge of the news item. Figure 3-12 shows the result.

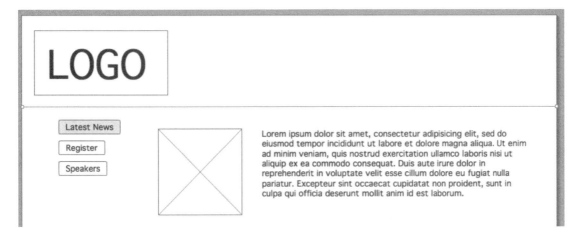

Figure 3-12. News item layout

9. Duplicate the elements of the news item so you can better see what the page would look like with multiple news items. To do so, select the elements and use copy (Ctrl-C) and paste (Ctrl-V). See Figure 3-13.

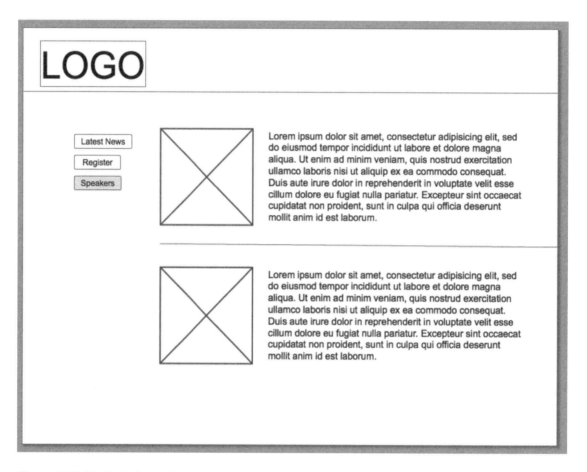

Figure 3-13. Duplicated news item

This wraps up the first state/page. Because many of the elements of the design in the first state are also in the second, you use the first as a base.

10. Click Duplicate State in the Pages/States panel (see Figure 3-14), and rename the new state **register**. Delete the news items to make room for other elements.

Figure 3-14. State duplicated and renamed register

This area lets you play with the other types of components that are available in Catalyst. Figure 3-15 shows an example of the kind of registration layout you can create in this page. You should be less concerned with the particulars of the layout than with the use of specific components. The set of wireframe components includes a good diversity of the most common interface elements but definitely not all you may require. Chapter 9 looks at creating custom components, but for now, let's get acquainted with the components that are predefined.

The layout in Figure 3-15 uses the Text Input, Check Box, and Radio Button components along with the text objects and drawn elements you're already familiar with. To maintain the speed and generic look of the wireframe, they're all placed on the stage with their default appearance.

The Text Input component is relatively straightforward. It has only two states: Normal and Disabled (see Figure 3-16).

The Check Box and Radio Button components have a similar structure and functionality but with one critical difference. When you place check boxes on the stage, they act independently of each other, allowing any or all of them to be checked at one time. On the other hand, radio buttons act as a set: only one radio button in a set can be selected at any given moment. To have two sets of radio buttons, you need different radio button groups (see Figure 3-16).

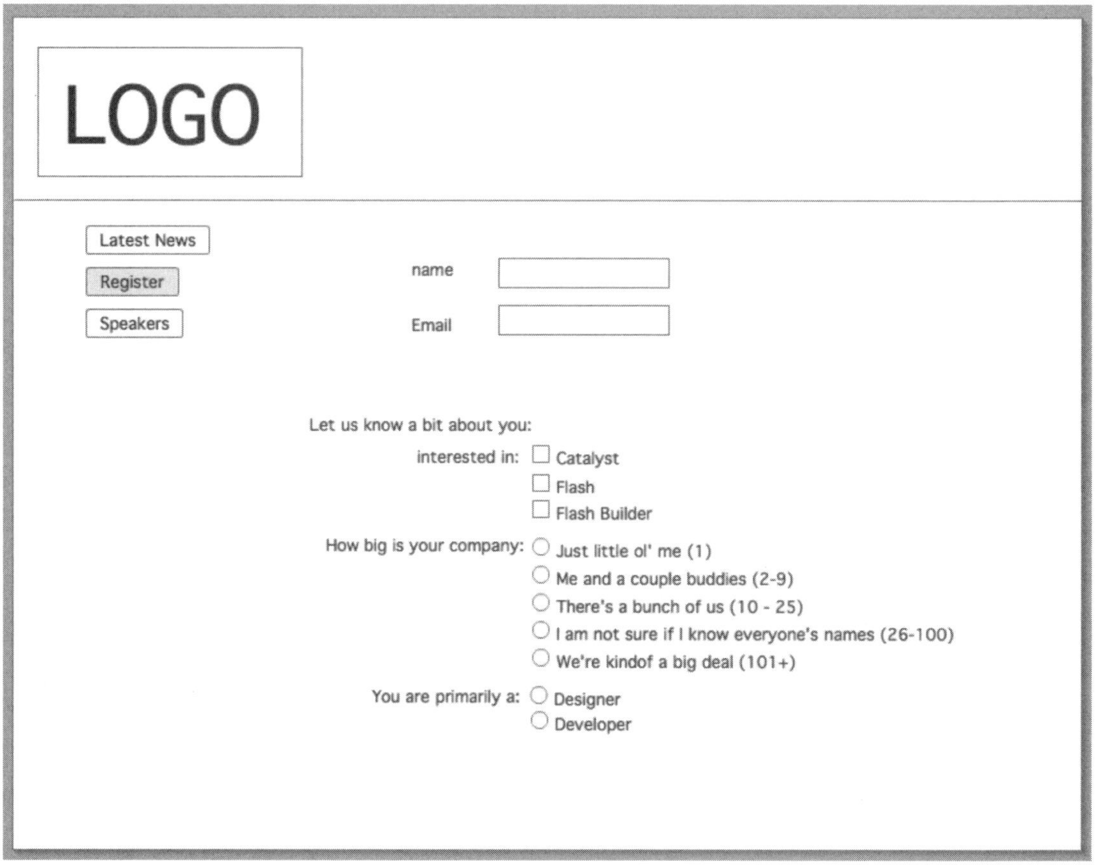

Figure 3-15. Layout of wireframe components for the register state

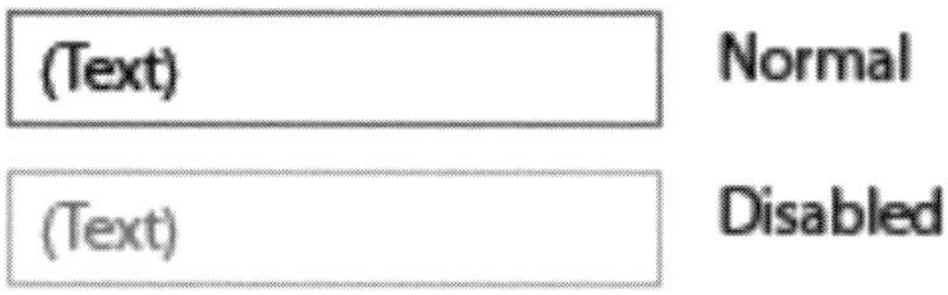

Figure 3-16. Text Input component states

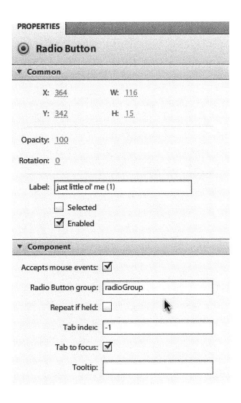

Figure 3-17. Creating a radio button group in the Properties panel

11. Make the Register toggle button selected and the Latest News toggle button not selected. Doing so highlights the Register button whenever the user is on this state.

The third state you need to create is the Speakers page. This page uses the most versatile of Catalyst's components: the Data List component.

12. Duplicate the register state, and rename it **speakers** (see Figure 3-18). Delete the elements you created on the registration page.

Figure 3-18. Register state duplicated to create the speakers state

In most applications, you create lists of some kind. You generally need to sort relevant information and group this information in a logical order. You may group together, for example, names, pictures, numbers, prices, and so on, or even a combination of these mixed together. This is why Catalyst provides the Data List component.

The Data List component is highly useful and versatile because it can take simple elements and components and repeat them, creating a more sophisticated component. You can create design-time data, giving the impression of having live data in the prototype. This component is also useful for creating more complex navigational elements, as you explore in Chapter 7. In this example, you use a data list to create a list of the speakers.

13. Create a single speaker entry using the drawing and text tools, as shown in Figure 3-19. Again, Lorem Ipsum text is fine for the content.

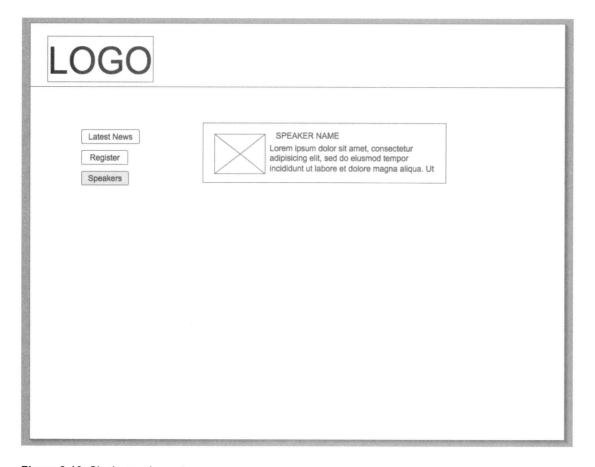

Figure 3-19. Single speaker entry

14. Select all the elements for the speaker entry, and in the HUD, select Convert Artwork to Component ➤ Data List (see Figure 3-20).

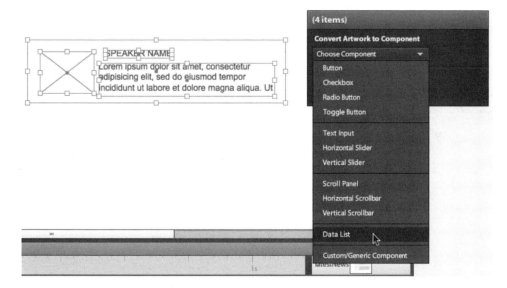

Figure 3-20. Speaker entry elements converted into a data list

15. The data list needs to know more about what in the selection should be repeated. The HUD is very useful at this point, because it guides you through the process. In the HUD, select Edit Parts; you find yourself inside the Data List component.

16. Select all the elements. In the HUD, select Convert to Data List Part ➤ Repeated Item (Required), as shown in Figure 3-21. Doing so creates a set of five copies of all the elements you selected. The contents of those elements are also placed in the Design-Time Data panel at the bottom of the interface, next to the timeline.

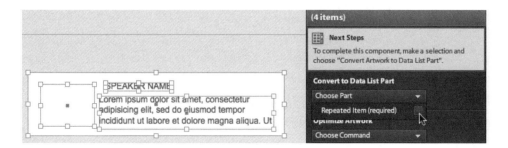

Figure 3-21. Defining data-list parts

The list in the Design-Time Data panel shows all the elements that are repeated. You can change these values manually by double-clicking any of the fields. You can modify text as well as images. When you click an image, you're offered the option to select another image from the library. Keep in mind that all of this data is for simulation only—the developer will replace these values with dynamic data later in the development process.

Data lists also offer the possibility of adding a scrollbar from a custom component.

Because the data list is the most sophisticated of the components, many properties and tricks are involved with its use; Chapter 7 looks at these in detail. For this example, you can stick with the default settings (see Figure 3-22).

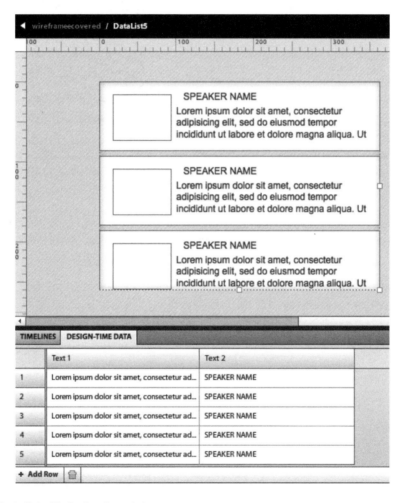

Figure 3-22. Data list with design-time data

17. Expand the bounding box of the Data List component so that all the elements are visible (see Figure 3-23). On this page/state, make sure the Speakers toggle button is selected. Now is also a good time to add the interactions to the toggle buttons to navigate through the states.

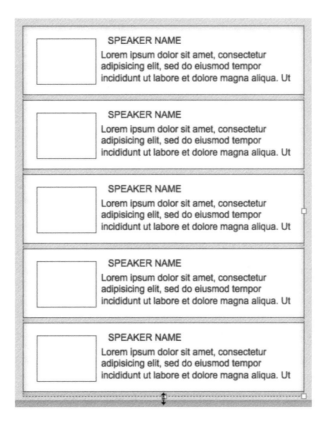

Figure 3-23. Data list with all five repeated items visible

18. To create an interaction for a button, select the button, and, in the Interactions panel, click Add Interaction. Select the appropriate state name from the Choose State pull-down menu, as shown in Figure 3-24.

19. Repeat this process for each of the three toggle buttons. Then, run the project (File ➤ Run Project).

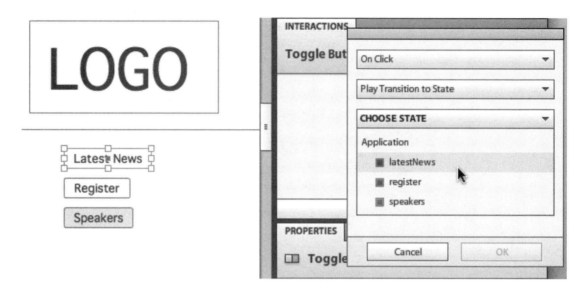

Figure 3-24. Interactions settings for the Latest News toggle button

So far, you've created a wireframe that shows the sections of the application and the layout of the major elements. In the next section, you add motion to the wireframe.

Adding Motion to the Wireframe

The repeated items in the Data List component have an Over effect. This indicates that the data list can have interactions associated with it. In this example, you create an expanded version of the speaker information: you add movement to the transition, because the user is affected by how the expanded information appears. Follow these steps:

1.   Duplicate the speakers state, and name it **speakersExtended** (see Figure 3-25).

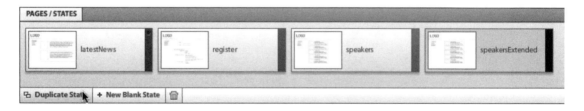

Figure 3-25. Speakers state duplicated to create the speakersExtended state

2. In this state, move the data list over to create a bit of space, and create a layout for the expanded speaker information using the drawing and text tools as shown in Figure 3-26.

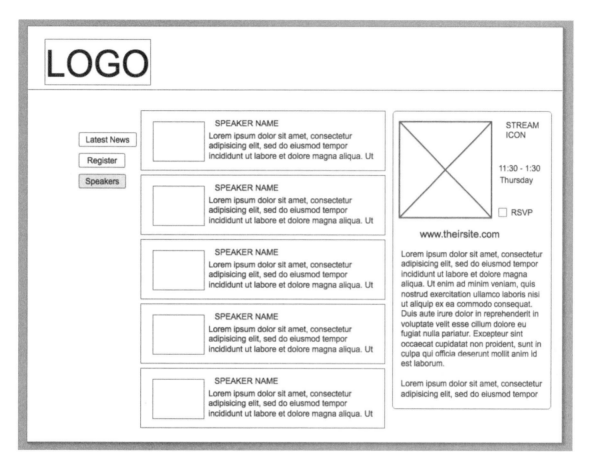

Figure 3-26. Layout of the speakersExtended state

For the animation, you want to create the impression that the expanded information about the speakers is coming out from behind the data list. This involves a fade and a change in x position. A fade is available pretty universally for the elements in Catalyst; but to create a change in position, you need a starting point and an ending point. The ending point is the location of the elements in the state you're transitioning to, whereas the starting point is the location of the elements in the state you're transitioning from. Because the elements currently exist only in the speakersExtended state, you need to also place them on the speakers state. This situation comes up quite often in Catalyst, and the developers at Adobe created an easy way to copy elements to other states.

3. Select all the elements that make up the expanded information for the speaker, and right-click them. Select Share To State ➤ speakers (see Figure 3-27). This places the elements into the speakers state, where you can modify how you want them to appear at the start of the animation. Specifically, you want to move them behind the data list and change the Opacity to 0.

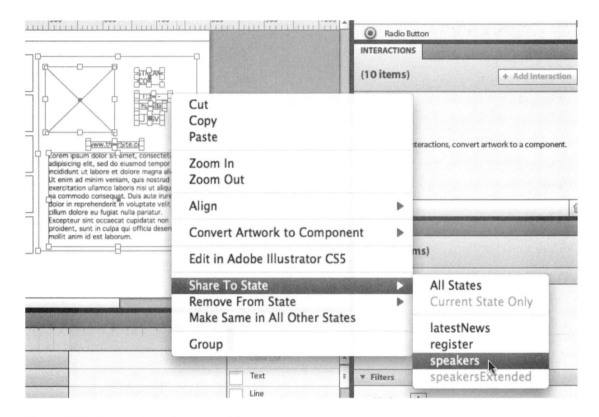

Figure 3-27. Sharing elements across states

4. To smooth the transition between the speakers state and the speakersExtended state, open the Timelines panel at the bottom of the interface. In the list of timelines, select speakers ➤ speakersExtended, and click Smooth Transition.

Figure 3-28. Smoothing the transition between the speakers and speakersExtended states

5. Add to the data list an interaction to transition to the speakersExtended state, using the same technique you used for the toggle buttons earlier in the chapter.

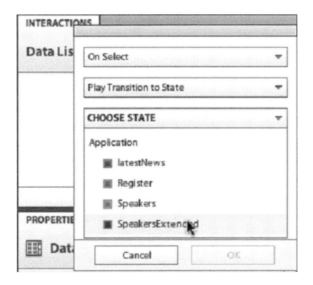

Figure 3-29. Interactions for the data list

6. Run the project.

Conclusion

When you've had some practice with wireframing, creating a wireframe like this should take you about an hour. Much more than that, and you're likely making it too much like the final product; and much less than that, and your mouse might catch fire! The emphasis is on illustrating ideas quickly and being able to share them quickly. Because Catalyst allows you to create wireframes so quickly, you can create more of them, and you don't become overly tied to your first ideas. The more ideas you have at the beginning stage of your design phase, the better the final results are likely to be.

Note that Adobe Flash Catalyst may not necessarily have wireframe components to suit all your needs. You may also want to create custom images to serve as place holders, or use the drawing tools to quickly create your own wireframe components.

Wireframes are meant to test ideas. After you've decided on a design, it's generally better to start with a clean file in Illustrator or Photoshop and create the prototype as you did in Chapter 2, rather than trying to add graphics to a wireframe. This may seem surprising—Catalyst allows for the very quick creation of components from graphics, but it can be cumbersome to add graphics to wireframes

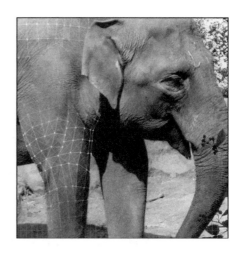

Chapter 4

Animation in Catalyst

What we'll cover in this chapter:

- Animating across states using transitions
- Tweaking transitions
- Adding custom actions to transitions
- Creating actions sequences

Files used in this chapter:

- animationExample-start.fxp
- animationExample-complete.fxp

Catalyst is very good at giving you the ability to quickly add animation to a design. This reinforces how the application ultimately responds to the user. It also allows you to finely control and define how the objects respond, rather than passing that work on to the developer.

Animation in Catalyst is primarily done by controlling the changes in object properties across states. If an image is in one position in the first state and in a different position in the second state, you can animate how the image moves between those two positions. This is true of transitions across the application's primary states and in components (such as rollover effects). You can also create animation separate from state transitions by creating action sequences. This chapter looks at all of these topics.

To work through the various kinds of animation features that are available, in this chapter you create an example of a simple interactive magazine layout. You can see the final example at www.greggoralski.com/ animationExample (see Figure 4-1) or look at final Catalyst file, animationExample-complete.fxp.

Figure 4-1. Final project

This file has a series of different types of animations including, in the order you create them, rollover and click animations for the three buttons, a state-change animation when the surfButton is clicked, a state-change animation involving 3D rotation, and a series of fade-in effects on the front page that are action sequences.

Animating Buttons

One of the most common uses of animation in interface design is the creation of rollover and click effects. These can guide users through the interface and let them clearly see when something has been triggered.

To begin this exercise, open animationExample-start.fxp. You can begin with a blank file if you wish, but this one has a collection of objects in the Library that lets you move more quickly through the example and concentrate on the elements that are important for animation. Look through the file before you begin:

it's relatively straightforward, with nothing created on the stage but a variety of objects in the Library. These include buttons, custom components, images, and audio, as shown in Figure 4-2.

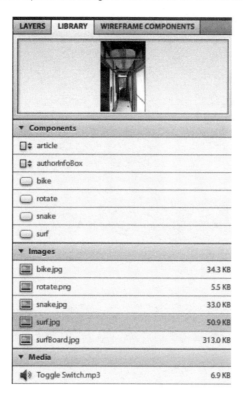

Figure 4-2. Library of animationExample-start.fxp

You begin by creating an animated button from a static image, in this case surf.jpg. Follow these step:

1. Drag an instance of surf.jpg onto the stage (see Figure 4-3). To drag an item out of the Library, select the name in the list and drag it onto the stage.

2. The HUD guides you to convert this image into a component. Select Convert Artwork to Component ➤ Button from the drop-down list (see Figure 4-4). Doing so wraps the image in a component (you can think of it as a movieClip if you've spent a lot of time designing in Flash) and gives it four distinct states (Up, Over, Down, and Disabled, as shown in Figure 4-5) along with the behavior of a button.

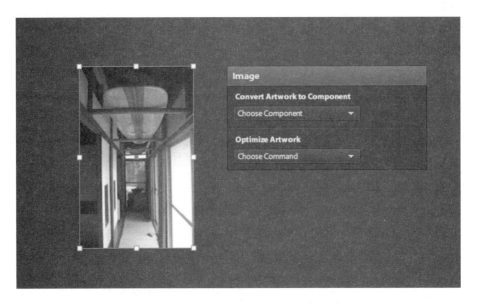

Figure 4-3. Image on the stage

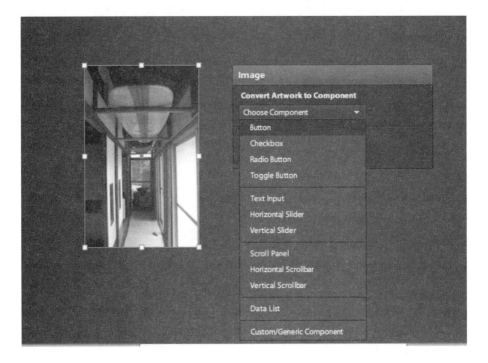

Figure 4-4. Converting an image into a button

Figure 4-5. States of the button

3. In each state, you draw how you want the button to look at that time. For now, leave the Up state as it is. Select the Over state, and use the Catalyst drawing tools to draw a box. In the box's Properties, set its stroke to None, the fill to black, and Opacity to 80. Using the Text tool, add text over the box as shown in Figure 4-6.

Figure 4-6. The Over state of the button, with a box and text added

At left in the Timelines panel is a list of all the possible transitions between the states—for example, from Over to Up. If you select Over,➤ Up all three of these transitional changes to the Over state are visible in the timeline (see Figure 4-7).

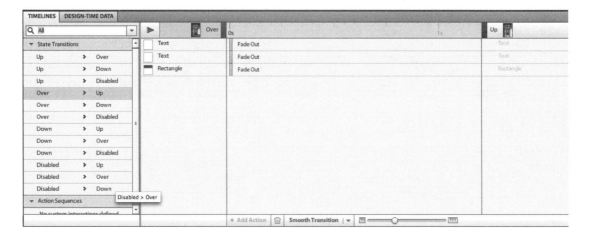

Figure 4-7. Timelines panel for the Over state to the Up state

The addition of the box and the two text fields are recognized as differences between the two states that can be animated. Catalyst automatically gives them the most appropriate change (in this case, because not all of the elements exist in the Up state, but they do exist in the Over state, the most appropriate change is a fade). At this point, the changes happen instantly. To make them animated, you need to provide them with a duration. To do so, drag them out (see Figure 4-8, fading the Up to Over state). By default, a timeline of 1 second is shown, but most animations are shorter.

Figure 4-8. Manually dragging out tbe length of an animation

Alternatively, you can click Smooth Transition (see Figure 4-9). Doing so gives a default half-second duration to all undefined animations in the selected state transition. You see how to modify these default settings when you use this technique to make transitions between the main states of a project.

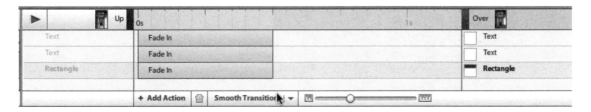

Figure 4-9. Controlling the length of an animation by clicking Smooth Transition

4. Click Smooth Transition, and then run the project to see how this works.

You've created your first rollover effect. Let's tinker with it a bit to see some of the options you can use to affect this transition. The box fades in nicely, but you want it to resize. This kind of effect needs the object to exist in the transition's starting and ending states. This makes logical sense: in order for something to resize, it must be there in the first place. The same applies for changes in position. You eventually have a variation of the box in every state of the button, so you may as well share it with all the states at this point:

5. To share the box with all the other states, select it and choose States ➤ Share to State ➤ All States (see Figure 4-10).You can also reach this command through the context menu by right-clicking the object you want to share.

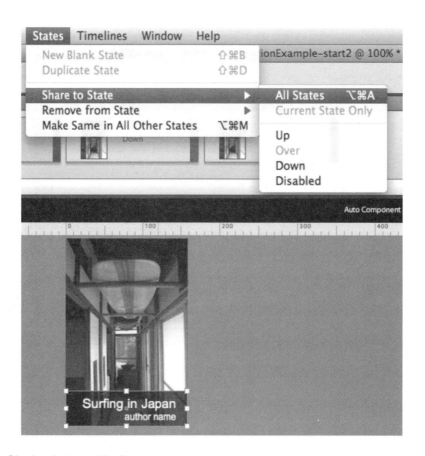

Figure 4-10. Sharing the box with all states

6. When you have a copy of the element that needs to change in all the states, you can modify it and smooth the state transitions. Let's start with the Up state. In the Pages/States panel, select the Up state, and scale the box vertically until it's invisible (you can scale a box down to have a height of 0, as shown in Figure 4-11).

Figure 4-11. Box with a height of 0

7. In the Timelines panel, select the Up ➤ Over state transition. You can see in Figure 4-12 that the rectangle exists in both states (it isn't faded out, because the text is in the Up state) and has a move and a resize change on the timeline. Click Smooth Transition to make these changes gradual over half a second, and then run the project.

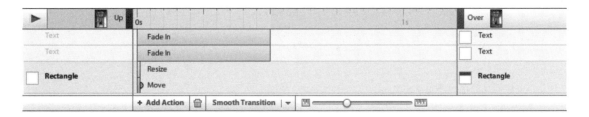

Figure 4-12. Timelines panel for the Up ➤ Over state transition before the transitions are tweaked

8. The animation is closer to what you're looking for, but it's awkward that the text appears before the box opens. You can manually modify the transition's start and duration by dragging the animations on the timelines. To make the texts fade in later than the start of the rectangle resize, move the times as shown in Figure 4-13.

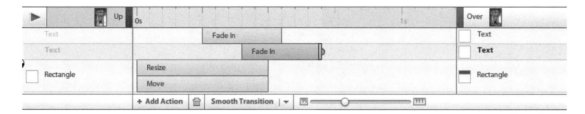

Figure 4-13. Timelines panel for the Up ➤ Over state transition after the transitions have been tweaked

9. To create the way the box and texts look in the other states, follow the same process: share the elements with the states as needed, modify the elements on each state in a certain way (for example, resize, change color, change opacity), and click Smooth Transition. To make the process less cumbersome, especially when many states are involved, select all of the state transitions and click Smooth Transitions (see Figure 4-14). Doing so inserts a default half-second of smoothing that you can then tweak.

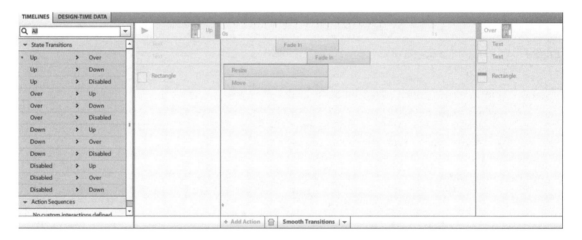

Figure 4-14. Timelines panel with all transitions selected

10. This example uses a trick. If you've tried the completed example, you may have noticed that after the surfButton is clicked, it stays highlighted, reinforcing for the user where they are in the navigation. To get this effect, create the Disabled state to look like a highlighted version of the button. As you build out the next state of the project, you control when the Disabled state is visible by using the button's Enabled property.

11. As a finishing touch, add an inner shadow to the button by selecting the button in the main state and then, in the Properties panel, selecting Add Filter ➤ Inner Shadow as shown in Figure 4-15. Note that a completed version of this button, called Surf, is available in the Library panel.

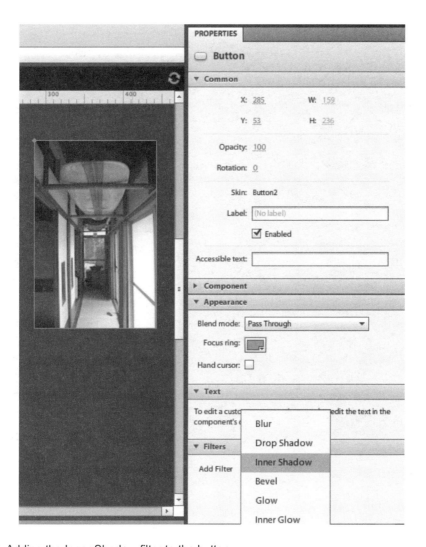

Figure 4-15. Adding the Inner Shadow filter to the button

12. Create the other two buttons using the same process, or use the buttons named Bike and Snake in the Library to save time. A trick to make the process of creating similar buttons faster is to duplicate buttons that you've already created and then modify them. You do this the same way you would in Flash. You can duplicate a button in the Library by right-clicking it and selecting Duplicate; this duplicate of the button can then be edited.

13. Arrange the three buttons in the first state (see Figure 4-16).

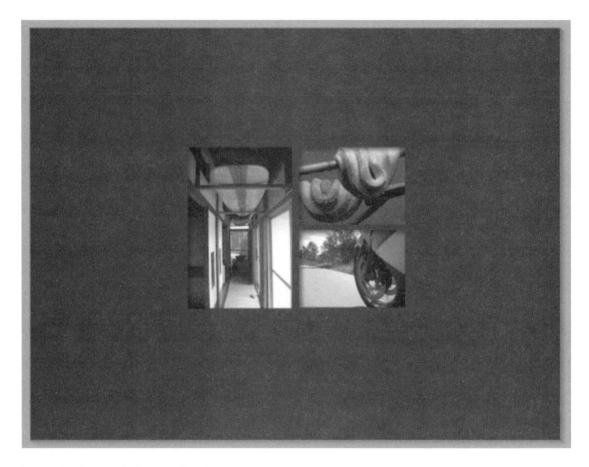

Figure 4-16. Three buttons on the stage

14. A new layer was automatically created for each button. To keep things clean and organized, name the layers as shown in Figure 4-17.

LAYERS	LIBRARY	WIREFRAME COMPONENTS	
👁			snakeButton
👁			bikeButton
👁			surfButton

Figure 4-17. Naming the layers that contain the buttons

Animating Across States

Catalyst uses the same logic when creating animations between the main states of a project that it does between the states of a button (or any other component). The significant difference with the main states is that they're created by the designer and tend to have more dramatic changes.

Almost all animations in Catalyst are between states. In this case, the animation you focus on is the transition from the cover to an article page—specifically, an article about surfing in Japan. If you look at the completed example, you can see that it involves the buttons moving to new positions while the article and background image fade in. (The article and the background image are in the Library and are named article and beach.jpg.)

To create the animation, follow these steps:

1. Because you're creating the states, begin start by naming the first state **cover** as shown in Figure 4-18.

Figure 4-18. Naming the first state

2. Duplicate the cover state, and name the duplication **surfArticle**.

3. In this new state, you can rearrange and add elements to create the look you want for the surfing article. Move the buttons as shown in Figure 4-19, and notice what happens on the Timelines panel: everything that is different between the two states is listed with the appropriate changes (in this case, Move; see Figure 4-20).

Figure 4-19. Repositioning the buttons in the surfArticle state

Figure 4-20. Timelines panel for the transition from surfArticle ➤ cover

4. Select the cover ➤ surfArticle state transition, and click Smooth Transition to spread the move over half a second. You can use the Play button to see how the animation runs. This button, which is close to the top of the Timelines panel, as shown in Figure 4-21, allows you to view a single transition; this is a quick way to get a sense of the animation.

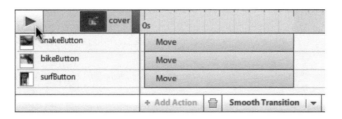

Figure 4-21. The Play button, which lets you preview animations

To change the easing of a movement, you can select the movement in the Timelines panel (you can also select multiple movements if required). The Properties panel shows the movement properties, including Duration, Delay, and Easing. By default, Catalyst has a relatively soft in/out easing that generally works quite well. The other options include the following:

- **Linear:** Easing acceleration and deceleration are at a constant rate. You can control the timing of the easing in and out.

- **Sine:** The ease accelerates to a mid point and then decelerates. This creates a movement that feels less artificial and stiff than a Linear ease. You can control the timing of the easing in and out.

- **Power:** Similar to Sine, because it accelerates to a midpoint; but it allows you to control the amount of acceleration and deceleration using the exponent value. The higher the exponent, the more dramatic the acceleration and deceleration. You can control the timing of the easing in and out.

- **Bounce and Elastic:** These options create either a bouncing animation or a rubber-band effect. Because these two easing styles have more movement, you should give them more time, or they look very unnatural.

5. Drag the background image, `beach.jpg`, and the surf article, `article`, from the Library onto the stage. `article` is a custom/generic component that contains a partially transparent rectangle and text fields containing the article and title. Custom/generic components are covered in Chapter 9; in this case, one is used very simply. The article component is merely a way to group the images and text involved in the article into a single component. Initially, the image and the article are on top of the buttons, as shown in Figure 4-22.

Figure 4-22. Article component and background image covering the buttons

6. In the Layers panel, move the layers containing the article and the background image below the buttons, as shown in Figure 4-23.

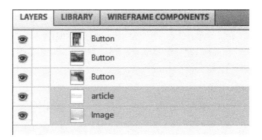

Figure 4-23. Article and image layers dragged below the button layers

With these elements on the stage, you can take a closer look at the default smooth transition you've been working with. Clicking the button to the right of Smooth Transition opens a menu that allows you to modify the default animation settings (see Figure 4-24).

Figure 4-24. Smooth Transition Options dialog box

In this dialog box, you can define the duration and also the type of timing to use. Simultaneous runs all the effects at the same time, whereas Smart Smoothing runs the animations for elements that exist in the opening state before starting the transitions on the elements that only exist in the finishing state. This change to the default settings becomes the new setting for the Smooth Transition button, allowing you to use these settings for subsequent transitions.

7. Use the default settings to complete this transition. The design now has the look for two states defined, along with how the animation looks—but it doesn't yet have the interactions. The interactions control when the application changes states. As you saw in Chapter 1, you create them in the Interactions panel.

8. In the first state, select the surfButton. In the Interactions panel, click Add Interaction. Define the interaction as being On Click, Play Transition to State, surfArticle (as shown in Figure 4-25). When you created this button, you gave it a visual for all the states, including the Disabled state. This state serves as your highlighted version.

Figure 4-25. Interactions panel settings for the surfButton

9. In the surfArticle state, select the surfButton. In the Properties panel, uncheck Enabled. Test the animation by selecting File ➤ Run Project in the main menu.

The project should now play the animation when you click the surfButton. To make the other buttons work, repeat the same process for each one.

3D Flip: Adding Actions to the Animations

Although most animations in Catalyst are between states, you can add other animation during a transition. In this example, you add a 3D flip to a normal transition. It's an example of how you can add actions to an existing animation to add complexity.

You can see this effect in the finished project: it's triggered by the Rotation button on top of the surfButton. When the Rotation button is clicked, the surfButton flips like a playing card to reveal a description on the back. The placement of the rotation button is shown in Figure 4-26.

Figure 4-26. Surf button with the Rotation button

As before, this is a transition between two states, so the first step is the creation of new state based on surfArticle:

1. Duplicate the surfArticle state, and name the duplicate surfFlipped. This gives you a new state exactly the same as the surfArticle state. No changes are available in the timeline, but you can add to it.

Figure 4-27. surfArticle state duplicated to create the surfFlipped state

2. Select the surfArticle ➤ surfFlipped transition in the Timelines panel. With the surfButton selected, click Add Action at the bottom of the Timelines panel, as shown in Figure 4-28.

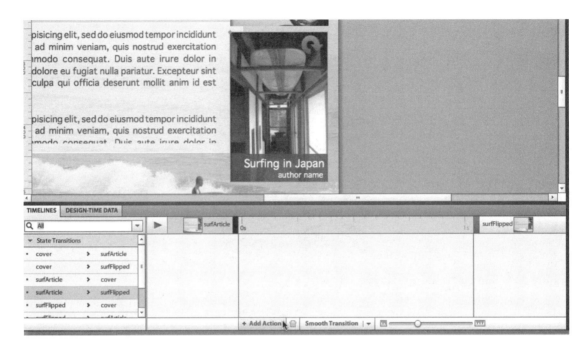

Figure 4-28. Clicking Add Action for the Surf button between states

3.   In the list of options are a variety of properties along with SWF, Video, and Sound effects. (Chapter 8 looks at these.) Select Rotate 3D, as shown in Figure 4-29. Doing so creates a 3D rotation movement on the timeline, as shown in Figure 4-30.

Figure 4-29. Add Action menu

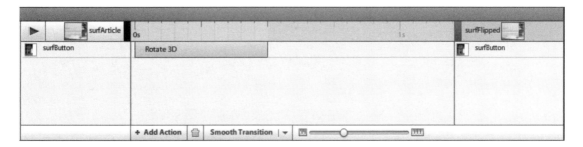

Figure 4-30. 3D rotation on the timeline

4. Selecting the 3D rotation lets you see its properties in the Properties panel. You can set how much and along which axis your want the rotation to occur, along with easing and delay if you choose. For this effect, the surfButton needs to rotate halfway (180 degrees) along the x-axis. Set the rotation as shown in Figure 4-31.

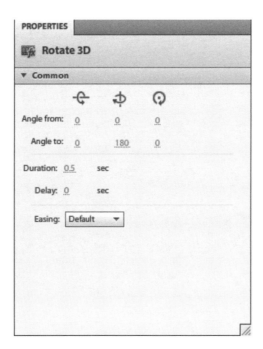

Figure 4-31. Rotation settings in the Properties panel

5. Play the animation by clicking the Play button in the Timelines panel to see the effect so far. You see the button rotating in 3D space. Note that even though you're rotating it, it still ends in the same position at the end (because that is how it's defined in the state).

101

6. The other half of this effect is the author information that's displayed. To save time, the Library contains a generic component named authorInfoBox that holds the author info. Drag an instance of authorInfoBox directly on top of the surfButton in the surfFlipped state. As shown in Figure 4-32, this creates the appearance of the button when it's flipped. This text is "on the back of the playing card" in this example's analogy.

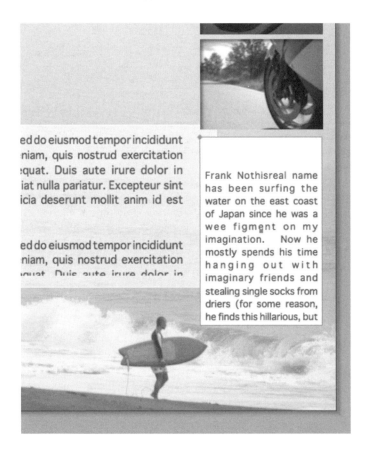

Figure 4-32. Author info placed on top of the Surf button

7. Select the authorInfoBox, and give it a 3D rotation using the same process but rotating from 180 to 360 degrees (see Figure 4-33). The difference is due to the card moving from being on its back to its front, so that it's face up in the surfFlipped state. You set this in the Properties panel.

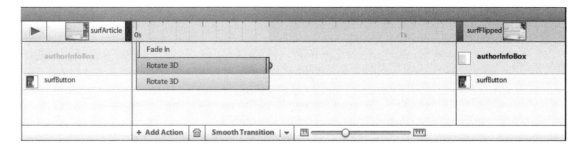

Figure 4-33. 3D rotation for the authorInfoBox

8. With the authorInfoBox, you can play the animation to see it working. Notice that the authorInfoBox stays on top of the surfButton the entire time. This is because there is no z-stacking in Catalyst (that is to say, the layer order doesn't change during transitions).

9. Because you only want the authorInfoBox to be visible halfway through the animation (when both objects are at 90 degrees to the viewer), move the fade in for the authorInfoBox to be halfway through the animation, as shown in Figure 4-34. This creates the flip animation going from the surfButton to the authorInfoBox whenever the project goes from the surfArticle state to the surfFlipped state.

> NOTE: Don't worry if you set up your action incorrectly, it's a simple thing to fix. In order to remove an action from the Timelines panel, select it and then click on the trash can icon at the bottom of the panel. You can then add the action again.

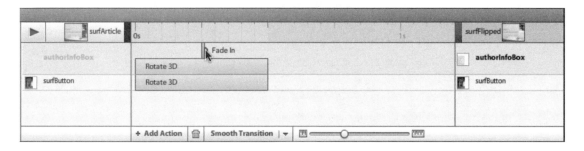

Figure 4-34. Fade in for the authorInfoBox moved to halfway in the transitions

10. Use the same technique to create the animation for the reverse flip (from authorInfoBox to surfButton) when the project goes from the surfFlipped state to the surfArticle state. The only difference is that this time, the surfButton needs to flip from 180 to 360 degrees (flip back), and the authorInfoBox goes from 0 to 180 degrees (flips over).

11. Create similar movements for the surfFlipped to surfArticle state transition using the same technique.

Controlling the Flip

To control the project's movement from the surfArticle state to the surfFlipped state and back, you need a button. This button is available in the Library; use the same technique you used to create the three main buttons. Then, follow these steps:

1. In the surfFlipped state, drag an instance of the Rotate button onto the authorInfoBox, as shown in Figure 4-35.

Figure 4-35. Rotation button on top of the authorInfoBox

2. In the Interactions panel, set the interaction for this button to On Click, Play Transition to State, surfArticle, When in surfFlipped (see Figure 4-36). Note the addition of When in surfFlipped. You do this because the button has a slightly different interaction when clicked in the surfArticle state, allowing the same button to jump back and forth between the two states. Run the project to test the effect by selecting File ➤ Run Project.

Figure 4-36. First interaction for the Rotate button

3. To have the same button flip the button back, share the button with the surfArticle state and, in the Interactions panel, add the interaction: On Click, Play Transition to State, surfFlipped, When in surfArticle (see Figure 4-37).

Figure 4-37. Second interaction for the Rotate button

Action Sequences

A final kind of movement that is possible in Catalyst is the action sequence. An *action sequence* is an animation or action that happens in a single state as opposed to between two states. Action sequences are triggered by some form of event, usually a click or the completion of the application load, but they don't need a change of state. Because of this, they can be useful in minimizing the number of states in a project.

An example of this kind of action sequence is the initial build of the navigation on load. To create any kind of action sequence, you first need to create the interaction that triggers it. The interaction that triggers the action sequence in this example is On Application Start, meaning that as soon as the application finishes loading, this action sequence begins.

Follow these steps:

1. Click anywhere on the application's background. This makes sure the application as a whole is the selected object in the Interactions panel. The Interactions panel now provides the options for adding an interaction to the application. The application can trigger only one kind of event: On Application Start. This event is triggered when all the application elements have been loaded.

2. In the Interactions panel, click Add Interaction to create the interaction. Define the interaction as being On Application Start, Play Action Sequence, as shown in Figure 4-38. This creates an empty action sequence below the list of state transitions in the Timelines panel (see Figure 4-39). You can place actions in this action sequence using the same technique you used to create the flip effect earlier in the chapter.

Figure 4-38. Interaction settings for the application

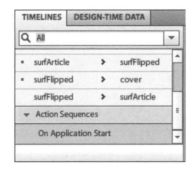

Figure 4-39. Empty action sequence created for On Application Start

3. The action sequence you create in this example is a fade in of the three buttons. To create the fades, in the cover state, select all three buttons (Surf, Bike, and Snake) and click Add Action (see Figure 4-40).

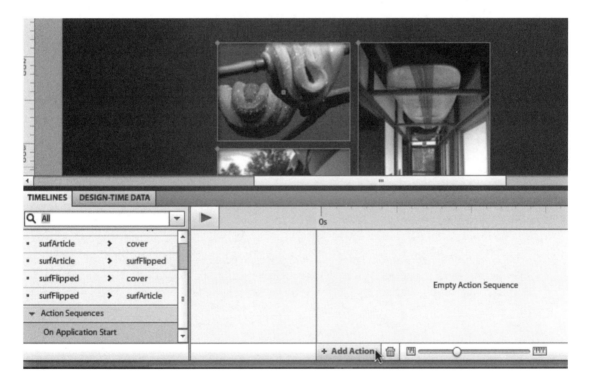

Figure 4-40. Adding an action to the three buttons

4. From the options that are presented, select Fade, as shown in Figure 4-41.

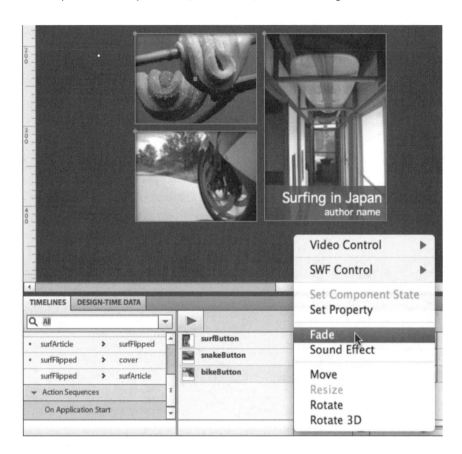

Figure 4-41. Adding the Fade action

5. By default, the Fade action fades out the selected objects. To have them fade in, use the Properties panel to set the Opacity of each button's fade to be from 0 to 100 (see Figure 4-42). This creates a fade effect for each of the three buttons when the application finishes loading.

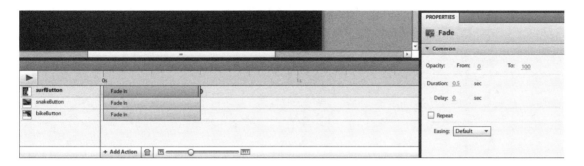

Figure 4-42. Properties for the fades

Conclusion

This chapter's example demonstrates the primary ways that animation works in Catalyst. You've seen how most animation in Catalyst is in the form of transitions, with elements changing from one state to the next. Catalyst is very effective at this kind of animation, allowing you to create appropriate transitions quickly using the Smooth Transition button in the Timelines panel. After you create animations, you can tweak them quite a bit.

This chapter also looked at another form of animation: additional actions and action sequences. Additional actions add a movement to an existing transition, and action sequences allow for animation without changing states.

The next chapter looks at how to best organize your assets when you're creating a Catalyst project.

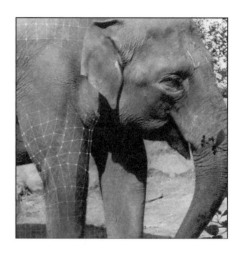

Chapter 5

Interactions

What we'll cover in this chapter:

- Working with the Interactions panel

- Using interactions in an application

- Using interactions in a video player

Files used in this chapter:

- `interactions-start.fxp`

- `interactions-complete.fxp`

Creating interactions in Catalyst is surprisingly direct and intuitive. This is partially due to Catalyst's focus has on the most common types of interactions, as opposed to trying to provide all possible options, and partially due to the intuitive design of the process. The Interactions panel responds to the type of object that is selected and guides you through the options specific to that component (although many interactions follow a similar pattern).

This chapter looks at how to use interactions to control state changes, trigger action sequences, control video, and open outside web sites. To explore these, you begin with the file `interactions-start.fxp` that is provided with this chapter. This file contains the series of buttons and video component shown in Figure 5-1, but no interactions yet. The design has been kept minimal so that you can focus specifically on the interactions. It contains two states: firstState and secondState. Both states are exactly the same with the exception of the text showing which state the user is currently in.

Figure 5-1. Starter file: `interactions-start.fxp`

Changing States

By far the most common use of interactions in Catalyst is to change states. Catalyst projects change states to move users through the different sections of a design. You create the states by duplicating a state in the States panel. The starter file provided with this chapter has two states created in it already. To create an interaction on a button, you select the button and then add the interaction in the Interactions panel:

1. Open the starter file `interactions-start.fxp`.

2. Select the first button, goToSecondStateButton. To create an interaction, in the Interactions panel, click Add Interaction to open a dialog box that is specific to that component type (see Figure 5-2).

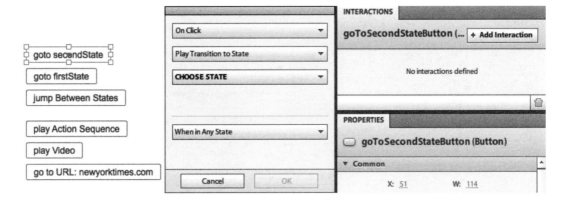

Figure 5-2. Setting interactions for gotoSecondStateButton

This dialog box provides a set of four (sometimes three) drop-down menus that allow you to define the interaction. The first of these deals with when the action is to occur (see Figure 5-3).

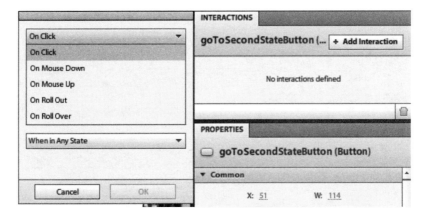

Figure 5-3. Setting when the interaction for gotoSecondStateButton is to occur

This drop-down gives you a set of the five most common types of interactions that are possible with the component. Most of these options are similar (for example, On Roll Over, On Roll Up, On Mouse Down, and On Mouse Up occur for all components), but some are specific to the component. For example, a button includes On Click; a data list includes On Select, as you see in Chapter 9; and a scrollbar includes

On Change. The one exception is an application, which only includes On Application Start. An example of the On Application Start interaction is shown later this chapter.

The next drop-down deals with what is to happen during this interaction (see Figure 5-4).

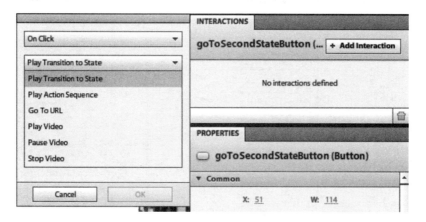

Figure 5-4. Setting what happens during the interaction for gotoSecondStateButton

The first of these, and the most common, is Play Transition to State; this is the interaction you set for the first three buttons in the example. Later, this chapter looks at each of these options.

The third drop-down defines which state to play to when Play Transition to State is selected. This drop-down lists all the main states in the project (see Figure 5-5).

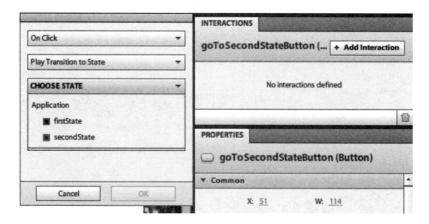

Figure 5-5. Setting the state to play to for gotoSecondStateButton

The fourth drop-down allows you to define the state in which this interaction is active (see Figure 5-6). The example's third button shows how this is useful.

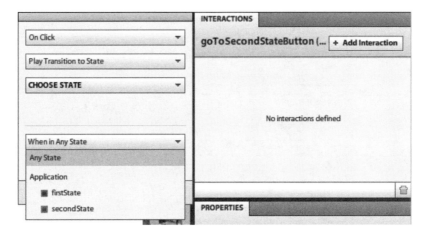

Figure 5-6. Setting the state in which this interaction is active

3. In goToSecondStateButton's Interactions panel, set the interaction to be On Click, Play Transition to State, secondState, When in Any State (see Figure 5-7). This creates an interaction that changes the application's main state to secondState.

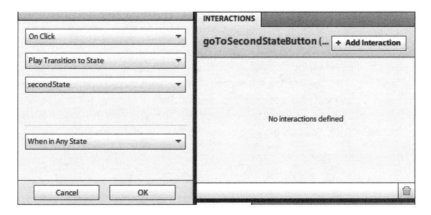

Figure 5-7. Interaction settings for goToSecondStateButton

To test this, run the project by selecting File ➤ Run Project in the main menu.

You can use the same technique to create the interactions for the second button, goToFirstState, allowing the user to return to the original firstState:

4. Select goToFirstStateButton and, in the Interactions panel, set the interaction to be On Click, Play Transition to State, firstState, When in Any State (see Figure 5-8).

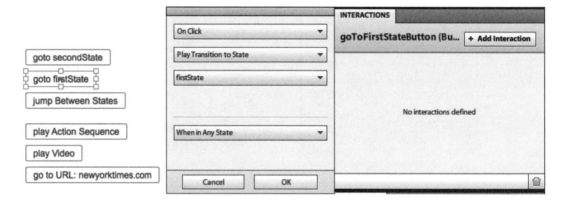

Figure 5-8. Interaction settings for goToFirstStateButton

Note that it doesn't matter which state the button is in when you create the interaction. A button's interactions are attached to the button itself, not to the state it's currently in. You don't, for example, have to add the interaction to secondState, even though that is where the interaction takes place.

To control whether an interaction occurs in a specific state, you use the last of the drop-downs in the add Interactions dialog box. This is useful if you want clicking a button to have a different effect depending on the state it's in. This is how you create the interactions for the third button, jumpBetweenStatesButton. As the name implies, this button lets the user jump to secondState if they're in the first, and to firstState if they're in the second. Because this is two interactions, you adding two interactions to the same button. It's possible to have multiple interactions on a single component.

5. Select jumpBetweenStatesButton, and, in the Interactions panel, click Add Interaction. Define the first interaction for this button as On Click, Play Transition to State, firstState, When in secondState, as shown in Figure 5-9. A click of this button transitions the user to secondState; but while in secondState, the button currently does nothing. For this reason, you need a second interaction.

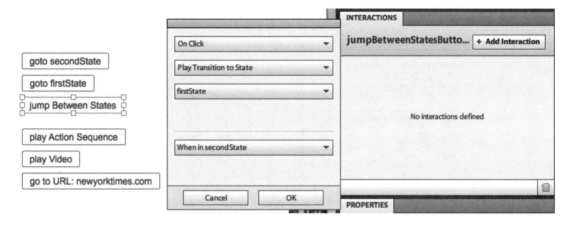

Figure 5-9. First interaction for jumpBetweenStatesButton

6. With jumpBetweenStatesButton selected, in the Interactions panel, click Add Interaction. Define this second interaction as On Click, Play Transition to State, secondState, When in firstState, as shown in Figure 5-10.

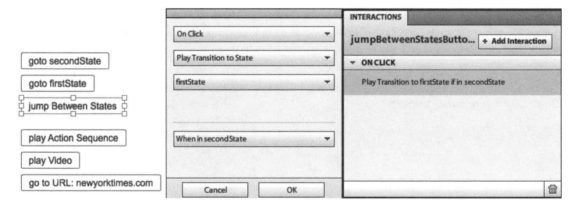

Figure 5-10. Second interaction for jumpBetweenStatesButton

117

You've now placed two interactions on the same button (see Figure 5-11). If there is a conflict between interactions on the same button, the one at the bottom, which is read last, overrides the earlier one. An example is shown in Chapter 9.

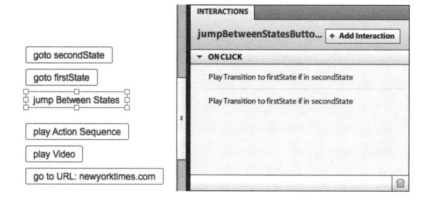

Figure 5-11. Multiple interactions on jumpBetweenStatesButton

Run this project to see how the interactions work in the project.

Triggering Action Sequences

The second major type of interaction that is triggered in Catalyst is the action sequence. As you saw in Chapter 4, an action sequence is a series of actions and animations that run in the current state. Chapter 4 showed how having an action occur while staying in a state can be useful and keep the number of states down. This is especially true if you're doing a simple animation onto a large number of items, such as a series of thumbnails.

To create an action sequence, you first define it in the Interactions panel and then add actions to it. Continue the example as follows:

1. Select playActionButton, and, in the Interactions panel, click Add Interaction. Define the interaction as On Click, Play Action Sequence, When in Any State (see Figure 5-12). Doing so creates an action sequence that is associated with this interaction in the Timelines panel (see Figure 5-13).

Figure 5-12. Interaction setting for playActionButton

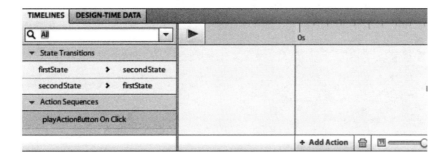

Figure 5-13. Action sequence in the Timelines panel for playActionButton

You can now add a variety of actions to the action sequence, including sound effects, 3D rotations, and SWF control. Chapter 4 looked at 3D rotation, and Chapter 8 examines sound effects and SWF control. To add an action to the action sequence, you select the object that is to be affected by the action and click Add Action at the bottom of the Timelines panel.

2. Select the video on the stage, and click Add Action in the Timelines panel. You can add a variety of different kinds of actions here, and Chapter 8 looks at most of them in detail: SWFs, video, and audio. To stay focused on interactions, add a simple Move action (see Figure 5-14).

Figure 5-14. Adding an action to an action sequence

Adding the move places the action on the timeline for the action sequence. To control the move, select it on the timeline, and change its properties in the Properties panel. By default, the move is 100 pixels down and 100 pixels to the right (see Figure 5-15). You can also define whether the move is relative or to a specific location. When it's defined as relative, a movement begins from wherever the object is. If you define the example movement as relative, it moves 100 pixels down and 100 pixels to the right every time the action is called until it can no longer be seen on the stage. When you define a move as being to a specific location, the X and Y coordinates define the exact location on the stage to which the object moves.

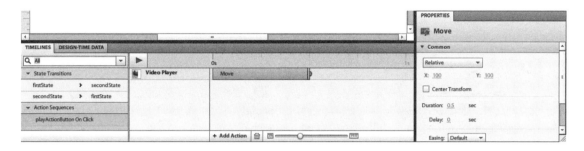

Figure 5-15. Properties for a Move action

You can add numerous actions to a single action sequence and control the timing and duration of the action in the timeline.

Controlling Video

Catalyst creates a video component when a video is imported. You can control this video component either in an action sequence, using the same technique you just used to add the Move action, or from the Interactions panel.

In this example, use playVideoButton to control the video:

1. Select the button on which the interaction will be placed, in this case playVideoButton. In the Interactions panel, click Add Interaction.

2. In this case, you want to play a video. Select Play Video in the second drop-down; a new drop-down appears that lets you define which video to play. Because only one video is imported into this project, only one is listed. The final interactions settings should look like Figure 5-16.

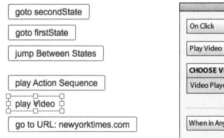

Figure 5-16. Video control through interactions

You can use the same technique to stop or pause the video.

Go To URL

The final interaction type available in Catalyst is Go To URL. This command allows you to open a file or site on interaction and control where it opens. In most cases, this takes the form of opening an outside site. In this example, you use gotoUrlButton to open the *New York Times* web site:

1. Select gotoUrlButton, and click Add Interaction.

2. In the options, select On Click, Go To URL. A text box appears in which you can enter the URL. For this example, enter **nytimes.com**.

3. The next drop-down lets you define where the site opens: Current Window, New Window, Parent Window (the window that opened the current one), or Top Window (the first window or frame that opened subsequent windows). The last two options are relatively obscure; most of the time, you open a site in either the current window or a new one. Select Open in New Window for this example. The resulting interaction settings look like Figure 5-17.

Figure 5-17. Interaction setting to open the *New York Times* web site in a new window

Interactions on the Application

Generally, interactions are placed on components and triggered by user interactions, but one kind of interaction trigger doesn't follow this model: interactions on the application itself. This particular type of interaction is triggered when the application load is complete. This is very useful when you want some kind of interaction to occur right at the beginning, such as playing a movie, animating the navigation system onto the screen, fading in images, and so on.

In this example, you use the On Application Start interaction to create an action sequence that fades in the video, but any kind of action is possible. To access the On Application Start interaction, click the stage away from any components. When nothing is selected, the Interactions panel defaults to showing the interactions for the application.

Continue as follows:

4. In the Interactions panel, click Add Interaction, and set the interaction to On Application Start, Play Action Sequence (see Figure 5-18). As you saw earlier this chapter, this creates an action sequence in the Timelines panel that allows you to add a variety of kinds of actions. The most common type of interaction on application start fades in the various elements on the stage. In this example, you fade in the video, but this technique works for any and all elements on the stage.

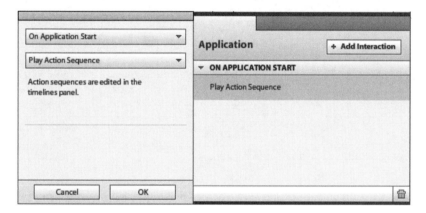

Figure 5-18. Interaction for the application

5. With the action sequence selected in the Timelines panel and the video selected on the stage, click Add Action ➤ Fade, as shown in Figure 5-19. This created a half-second fade for the video. By default, the fade goes from its current value to 0. Because you want the video to fade in, it needs to go from 0 to 100. You can set this in the fade's properties.

Figure 5-19. Adding a Fade action to the action sequence

6. To access the properties for the Fade action, select the fade in the Timelines panel. In the Properties dialog box, set the From value to 0 and the To value to 100, as shown in Figure 5-20.

Figure 5-20. Changing the properties of the Fade action

Run the project (File ➤ Run Project) to see the result. You first see the progress bar that starts all Catalyst projects. When loading is complete, the video fades in over half a second; the rest of the project appears instantly.

Conclusion

In this chapter's example, you've used a variety of different interactions; and, significantly, you've created them without a lick of code. The code is created automatically in the background, in the form of MXML. This allows the interaction designer to focus on creating the experience without needing to pull in a developer at this point.

The next chapter looks at Catalyst best practices so that when it's time for you to pull the developer into the project, the file is clear and usable for them.

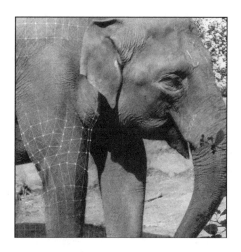

Chapter 6

Organizing Artwork and Best Practices

What you'll cover in this chapter:

- Naming conventions
- Organizing assets
- Optimizing graphics

Files used in this chapter:

- None

Because working with Catalyst involves passing files between multiple programs (Illustrator or Photoshop to Catalyst to Flash Builder) and between team members (designer to developer), keeping files organized and clear makes projects move much more smoothly. Looking at the way the files are structured is especially important as you prepare them to move from one application to the next. In this chapter, you look at some of the ways to do this.

The Golden Rule

The golden rule is to name everything. Elements that aren't named are given generic names in Catalyst, and those names don't help you understand the elements' relationship to other aspects of the project. This is true for states (as you saw in Chapter 4) as well as layers and components. Names given to layers in Illustrator or Photoshop are carried over into Catalyst, so it's a good idea to start your naming process there.

As you prepare to move your artwork from Illustrator to Catalyst, take some time to organize your layers so they make logical sense in Catalyst. First, place all the states and functional parts into separate layers. This allows you to easily make visible or invisible whole sections of the interface as you create project states in Catalyst.

Layers should be logically grouped using descriptive names. For example, if you're creating a button, you should have a folder called `Button`, and inside it should be layers with the Up, Over, Down, and Disabled states, as shown in Figure 6-1.

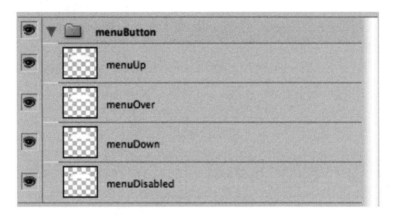

Figure 6-1. Layer-naming convention for graphics to be made into a button

To keep things clear and understandable, it's a good idea to follow the same naming conventions as in the wireframe components. For example, when you're creating a button, follow the naming convention used for a button's states, as shown in Figure 6-2.

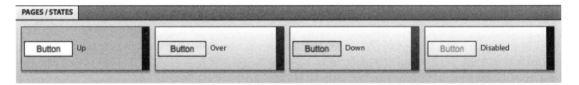

Figure 6-2. States of a button

When you're naming layers that contain entire components, it's a good idea to follow a naming convention that's easy for developers to understand. This involves descriptive names that follow camelCase naming conventions. For instances of a component, camelCase naming involves starting with a lowercase letter and then capitalizing the first letter of every new word in the name, without using any spaces. Examples include `menuButton`, `formButton`, and `nameInputText`. This method is clear to read while also defining what the component is used for. This is a standard method, although if you prefer, you and your team can agree on a different naming convention.

While in Flash Catalyst, you can look in the code view to see how the names you assign to your layers are used in the code generated in the background. To do this, select Code from in the view pull-down in the top-right corner of the interface (see Figure 6-3).

Figure 6-3. Switching to code view

This view shows all the files created for the project. Each component is given its own file in the Components folder (see Figure 6-4).

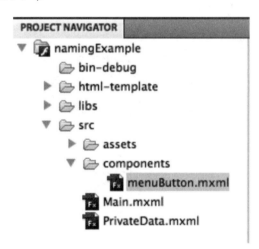

Figure 6-4. File containing code for a button

Double-clicking a file opens the code that has been generated. Figure 6-5 shows the code that is generated for simple custom buttons.

```
Main.mxml ⊗   menuButton.mxml ⊗
 1  <?xml version="1.0" encoding="utf-8"?>
 2⊖ <s:Skin xmlns:s="library://ns.adobe.com/flex/spark" xmlns:fx="http://ns.adobe.com/mxml/2009" xmlns:d="http://ns.adobe.com/fxg/2008/dt" xmlns:ai="http://ns.adobe.com/ai/2009">
 3⊕    <fx:Metadata>[HostComponent("spark.components.Button")]</fx:Metadata>
 4⊖    <s:states>
 5          <s:State name="up"/>
 6          <s:State name="over"/>
 7          <s:State name="down"/>
 8          <s:State name="disabled"/>
 9      </s:states>
10⊖    <fx:DesignLayer d:id="2" d:userLabel="menuButton">
11          <s:BitmapImage ai:embed="1" height="95" smooth="true" source="@Embed('assets/images/button/disabledButton.png')" d:userLabel="disabledButton" width="348" x="0" y="0" v
12          <s:BitmapImage ai:embed="1" height="95" smooth="true" source="@Embed('assets/images/button/downButton.png')" d:userLabel="downButton" width="348" x="0" y="0" visible.d
13          <s:BitmapImage ai:embed="1" height="95" smooth="true" source="@Embed('assets/images/button/overButton.png')" d:userLabel="overButton" width="348" x="0" y="0" visible.d
14          <s:BitmapImage ai:embed="1" height="95" smooth="true" source="@Embed('assets/images/button/upButton.png')" d:userLabel="upButton" width="348" x="0" y="0" visible.over=
15      </fx:DesignLayer>
16⊕    <s:transitions>
31  /s:Skin>
32
```

Figure 6-5. Code for a button in code view

A developer can easily read this code largely because the naming used is clear and consistent. Looking at the first line in the design layer (line 11), for example, it's obvious that this represents the button's disabled state, because the code brings in an image file named disabledButton.png, and which has been given the user label disabledButton. The name for the image file comes from the name you give it in the Library panel (see Figure 6-6), and the user label is the layer name.

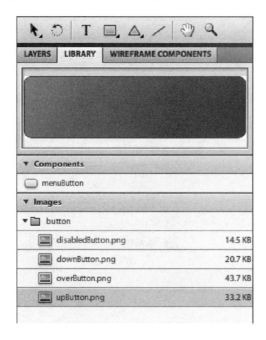

Figure 6-6. Naming of images in the Library panel

It's a good idea to scan through the code view, looking for generic names. When you find one, it's much easier for you to change the name in Catalyst than it is for a developer to guess what it the component is.

Organizing Assets in Fireworks

Although Catalyst can't import Fireworks files directly, this doesn't prevent people who design in Fireworks from getting in on the action. But bringing in a file from Fireworks involves the additional step of exporting to FXG format first. FXG is an XML-based file format that lets you transfer files across programs in the Flash platform. The Illustrator and Photoshop files you've been bringing into Catalyst are also converted to FXG. The main difference is that Catalyst can convert these files when they're imported into Catalyst, whereas Fireworks files need to be exported into the format.

The advantage of Fireworks over the other primary graphics programs is that it can create *pages*. These pages are retained in the FXG format and become states/pages in Catalyst.

To export to FXG from Fireworks, follow these steps:

1. Create a design using the graphics tools in Fireworks, making sure you use clear and consistent naming for the layers and pages.

2. From the main menu, select File ➤ Export (see Figure 6-7).

Figure 6-7. Exporting in Fireworks

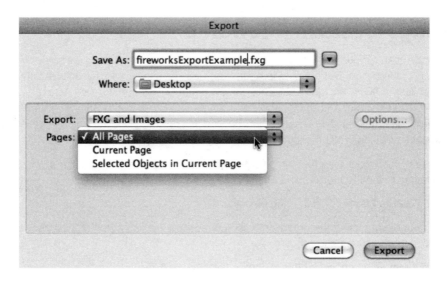

Figure 6-8. Fireworks Export dialog box

fireworksExportExample.fxg	Today, 7:20 PM	16 KB	FXG File
▶ fireworksExportExample.assets	Today, 7:20 PM	--	Folder

Figure 6-9. Exported files

Note that use of components in Fireworks' common libraries isn't supported. They're brought into Catalyst as optimized graphics rather than as functioning components.

Organizing Assets in Illustrator

One of the main advantages of working with Adobe Illustrator to create your original comp is its emphasis on vector graphics. Because vector information can be represented with the FXG format, it remains editable in Catalyst. Vectors can also be scaled without pixelating.

There are some things to consider when using Illustrator. In order to keep your files simple and make them easier to transport, you should embed all images into the files rather than having them linked. When you're passing files to other team members, it's easier to lose track of linked images than embedded images.

If you use special fonts, evaluate when the fonts used in your design could be outlined. This avoids bloating the project by embedding too many fonts and makes the representation of your fonts more consistent. This is particularly true for type that has filters and effects applied to it—Catalyst can usually represent it consistently, but not always. Keep in mind that text that has been outlined isn't editable.

Complex artwork should be grouped and flattened onto as few layers as possible. Because most of the art you create is made up of multiple layers that aren't modified in Catalyst, a single flattened layer is easier for you to work with in Catalyst and much easier for the developer afterward. The exception is when you plan to modify parts of that artwork—for example, if a text box changes depending on the use or state of the component to be built from the artwork.

The following Illustrator filters and effects are supported in Catalyst:

- Drop Shadow
- Inner Glow
- Outer Glow
- Gaussian Blur

All other filters and effects are flattened or rasterized during the import process.

Organizing Assets in Photoshop

Assets in Photoshop are frequently created by combining several layers with different blend modes and effects. To keep the layers in Catalyst organized, it's useful to flatten layers in Photoshop when possible, leaving a single layer with a rasterized image. Flash Catalyst also rasterizes all layer effects for image, shape, and text layers from Photoshop during import.

When you're working with text layers that have effects or masks, you can use vector outlines or flatten the bitmap image to maintain a consistent appearance in Catalyst. When masks are applied onto a layer group, you need to flatten the bitmap image. Opacity changes on a layer group can be flattened to create a bitmap image.

Many blend modes don't transfer during the import into Catalyst and so need to be flattened to a raster image in Photoshop. These include the following:

- Vivid Light
- Linear Light
- Pin Light
- Hard Mix
- Lighter Color
- Linear Burn
- Darker Color
- Dissolve
- Divide

Using Multiple Instances of the Same Object

Regardless of which graphics program you choose to start your project in, you may find yourself creating identical graphic elements throughout your design. For example, your design may involve multiple instances of the same button. Because it's more efficient and easier to modify one version of a button that is used multiple times than it is to manage multiple versions, it's useful to mark these with a _copy suffix (see Figure 6-10). This way, in Flash Catalyst, you can easily delete these layers and reuse the same asset.

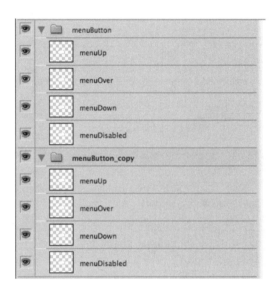

Figure 6-10. Menu button and a copy in the Layers panel

Defining Data List Components

Whenever you create a repeating set of items that will use live data in the final project, such as a gallery or product list, it's important to use a Data List component rather than create the items individually. It's much easier to replace the items in a Data List with live data, while maintaining the animations and behaviors you create for it in Catalyst, than it is to replace individual items.

Data List components, as you see in greater detail in Chapter 7 and again in Chapter 10, duplicate assets multiple times to create a set. Because Data Lists duplicate a similar set of assets (although modified), it's useful to create just one instance of the assets. Any others in the Illustrator or Photoshop file can be marked with the _copy suffix and then deleted in Catalyst. The parts of a Data List that change as the assets are duplicated (for instance, if you're creating thumbnails that involve different images for each thumbnail) should be included in layers nested in the assets for the Data List.

Optimizing Graphics

In Catalyst, you have the opportunity to affect your graphics after they're imported by using the Optimize Artwork commands in the Heads-Up Display (HUD) when an image or vector is selected (see Figure 6-11). Let's walk through each of your options.

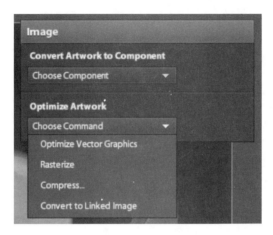

Figure 6-11. Optimize Artwork options

The Optimize Vector Graphics option allows you to select a variety of vectors and makes them into a single vector graphic that is then easier to manage. Vector graphics are seen as code in the MXML that is created in the background. This code can become complicated and difficult for the developer to work with. Figure 6-12, for example, shows how a rectangle with a gradient appears in the code.

```
<s:Rect height="179" width="190" x="160.5" y="46.5" d:userLabel="originalRectangle">
    <s:fill>
        <s:LinearGradient rotation="325.77" scaleX="242.714" x="-2.64648" y="155.995">
            <s:GradientEntry color="#ED4C14" ratio="0"/>
            <s:GradientEntry color="#FFD400" ratio="1"/>
        </s:LinearGradient>
    </s:fill>
    <s:stroke>
        <s:SolidColorStroke caps="none" joints="miter" miterLimit="10" weight="1"/>
    </s:stroke>
</s:Rect>
```

Figure 6-12. Gradient rectangle represented as MXML

Optimize Vector Graphics simplifies the main code file (main.mxml) for the developer by moving this complicated code into a separate file in the Assets/Graphics folder and putting a simplified placeholder in its place (see Figure 6-13). This is especially useful if the artwork is made up of multiple vector shapes.

Figure 6-13. Optimized graphic in MXML

The Rasterize option in the Optimize Artwork pull-down takes whatever is selected and rasterizes it at screen resolution in its current size. This is particularly useful when you're working with graphics that are considerably smaller than the original size you imported.

To see an example, look at the images used in Chapter 4 (see Figure 6-14). The surfBoard.jpg image is 313KB and 790 × 1200 pixels but is only used as a thumbnail image that's 159 × 235 pixels. After the image is scaled down to the size at which it's used, you can rasterize it using the Rasterize command. Doing so creates a new image in the library (named surf_1.jpg) that is 51KB. You can also use this option to convert vector graphics to bitmap images.

Figure 6-14. Images in the Library panel

The next Optimize Artwork option, Compress, allows you to further reduce an image's size, as shown in Figure 6-15.

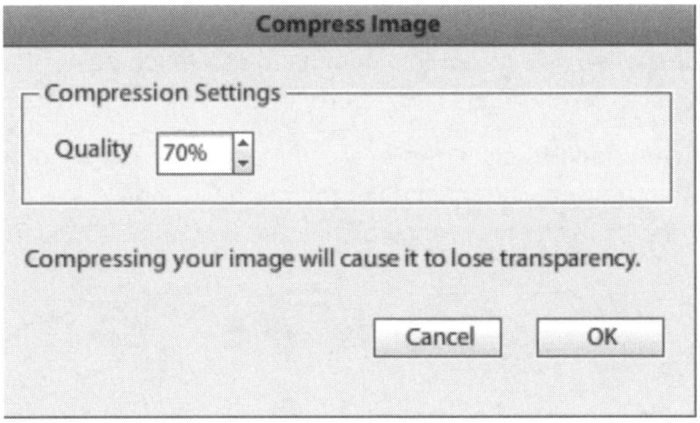

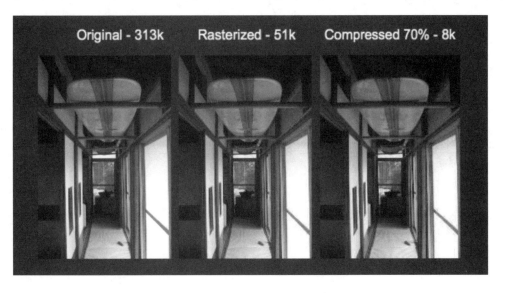

Figure 6-15. Image compression settings

Using the default compression setting of 70% compresses this image to 8KB. Again, a new image is created, this one named image1.jpg. It's a good idea to rename these images right away, using a clearer name.

At 100% scale, the differences between the three images are fairly slight, as shown in Figure 6-16. But of course you have to balance the relative importance of image quality and file size for your individual project.

Figure 6-16. Image with different Optimize Artwork settings at 100% scale

The final Optimize Artwork option, Convert to Linked Image, lets you make the selected image externally linked. Instead of placing the image into the SWF, this command saves the image into a folder called Assets/Images/ that is passed along with the project when it's opened in Flash Builder. This is particularly useful for large images such as galleries that you want to load externally and for which you want to include a preloader: when you select this command, it's much easier for the developer to add the preloader and for the images to be updated in the future.

From the design side, all you need to do is run this command. The file is automatically saved externally and kept associated with the project. The main difference that you notice in Catalyst is the addition of the folder icon to the listing in the Library. This is shown in Figure 6-17, next to the file size.

Figure 6-17. Linked image as shown in the Library

Round-Tripping

Round-trip editing allows you to bring images, vectors, and components into Illustrator or Photoshop so that you can use the tools in those programs to edit them easily and then quickly return to Catalyst. To round-trip between Catalyst and Illustrator, follow these steps:

1. In Catalyst, select the object you want to edit in Illustrator. This can be a single object, a mixed group of objects, or a component. You can only round-trip one component at a time, and custom/generic components can't be round-trip edited. Graphics that have been optimized by using the Optimize Vector Graphic command also can't be round-trip edited.

2. Select Modify ➤ Edit in Adobe Illustrator CS5, as shown in Figure 6-18. This opens Illustrator and shows your selection.

You can edit the selected items in Illustrator, along with their layer structure. The rest of the design appears as a faded image in the background and can't be edited (see Figure 6-19). Filters that are added in Catalyst can be edited in Illustrator, but filters that you add in Illustrator are converted to vectors or bitmaps on return to Catalyst.

Figure 6-18. Editing assets in Illustrator

Figure 6-19. Editing the Play button in Illustrator

3. When you've completed your edits, you can return to Catalyst by clicking Done at upper right on the artboard (see Figure 6-20).

Figure 6-20. Returning to Catalyst after editing in Illustrator

In a similar way, you can round-trip edit an image or a set of images in Photoshop. The difference is that Photoshop requires the FXG extensions. You can find them, along with installation instructions, at www.adobe.com/go/photoshopfxg.

To edit an image or a set of images in Photoshop, follow these steps:

4. Select the image. In the main menu, select Modify ➤ Edit in Adobe Photoshop CS5 (see Figure 6-21).

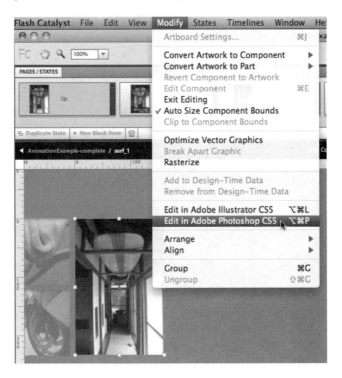

Figure 6-21. Editing an image in Photoshop

5. Catalyst reminds you that the FXG extensions for Photoshop need to be installed (see Figure 6-22).

Figure 6-22. Photoshop FXG extensions reminder

6. Click OK to open the image in Photoshop, again with the rest of the design faded in the background. From here, you can modify the image (see Figure 6-23).

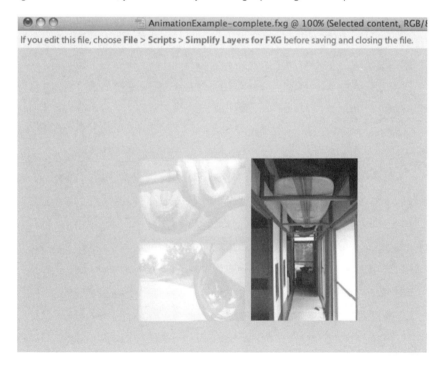

Figure 6-23. Image being edited in Photoshop

7. When you're finished with the edits, it's important to run the Simplify Layers script. This script simplifies some of the elements that Catalyst can't understand. For example, 3D layers and smart objects are rasterized and flattened by the Simplify Layers script. To run this script, select File ➤ Scripts ➤ Simplify Layers for FXG (see Figure 6-24). To return to Catalyst, save and close the Photoshop file.

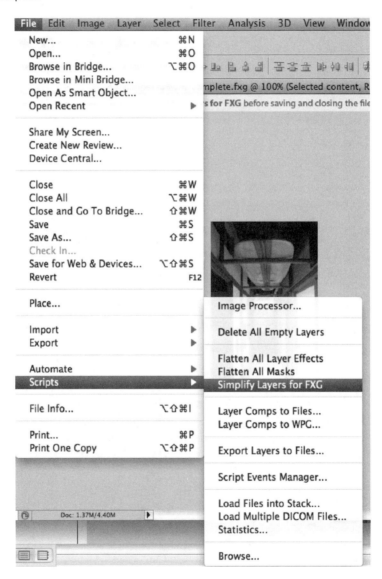

Figure 6-24. Simplify Layers for FXG script

Conclusion

It's difficult for a developer to take over a Catalyst project. Not only do they have to get up to speed with your design, but they must also manage a good deal of MXML that is automatically generated. You can see the MXML by switching to code view.

This code, because it's automatically generated, often requires a lot of manipulation to make it efficient and reusable. So, think beyond your needs in organizing the project, and be good to your developers: name everything descriptively, use camelCase, compress your images, keep the structure hierarchically organized, and, while you're at it, buy them a beer—they work hard.

It's a good idea to meet with one of your developers and go through the project while it's still in Catalyst. They can look at the code view and see areas where naming or structure can be changed to have a significant impact on their workload down the line.

The next chapter looks at how to use Data Lists and design-time data to create the impression of live data.

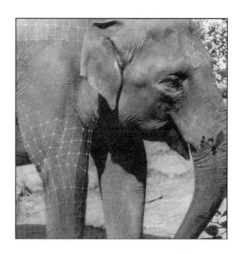

Chapter 7

Data Lists and Design-Time Data

What we'll cover in this chapter:

- Creating Data Lists

- Modifying design-time data

- Adding a horizontal scrollbar to a data list

Files used in this chapter:

- DataListAndDesignTimeData-complete.fxp

- Six images

Designing a site often involves using a repeated set of similar objects. This is true whether the repeated items are thumbnails in a gallery, posts in a blog, items on a product site, or dates on a calendar. Often, these repeated items are created based on external data from XML or server-side data. This is a mainstay of web design and makes for easily updatable and expandable pages. The challenge for the interaction designer at the start of a project is to create the look and behavior of the repeated items without requiring the outside data source to be created. Catalyst deals with this challenge through the use of Data Lists to repeat items and design-time data to give the impression that an outside data source exists.

Data Lists are components that repeat a set of objects a number of times to create a set. The simplest way to imagine this is to think about creating a photographer's site. Rather than individually creating each photograph thumbnail, you can create one and, using the Data List component, have it repeat as many times as you require. You can then control the layout of the thumbnails through the Data List component rather than manually repositioning all the thumbnails if the design changes. The Data List component allows you to change the orientation of the repeated items (such as horizontal, vertical, or tile) as well as the spacing between repeated items and the padding of the gallery as a whole. This makes it easier to create and modify your design; but more important, it makes it easier for the developer to connect your design with an external data source. Later in this chapter, you see how a developer can bring in the external data while maintaining the behavior and animation you create.

Design-time data allows you to modify the content of each repeated item so that it appears to be pulling from an external data source. To continue with the photographer site example, design-time data lets you change the image of each thumbnail easily to give the impression of a complete gallery rather than one repeated image. As you see in this chapter, this quick change of the content of the repeated item lets you make each one unique while maintaining any animation and behavior that you created on the first repeated item. The design-time data is later replaced with live data by the developer in Flash Builder.

In this chapter, you explore the Data List component and design-time data by creating a very simple bookstore prototype. The bookstore includes a series of repeated books complete with author name and information, rollover effects, scrollbar, and interaction. The visual appearance of this example is kept simple so it's easier to focus on how the Data List and design-time data function. The final result is shown in Figure 7-1. The completed project is provided with the files for this chapter.

Figure 7-1. Completed Data List with design-time data

Setting Up the Project

You begin by creating a new Catalyst project as you've done for previous examples:

1. In the initial dialog box, select Create New Project ➤ Adobe Flash Catalyst Project (see Figure 7.2). To keep things simple, use the default settings for the new project.

Figure 7-2. Catalyst initial dialog box

2. Import the six images that represent the books in your bookstore. These are the six JPG files provided with this example. Import them by choosing File ➤ Import ➤ Image, as shown in Figure 7-3.

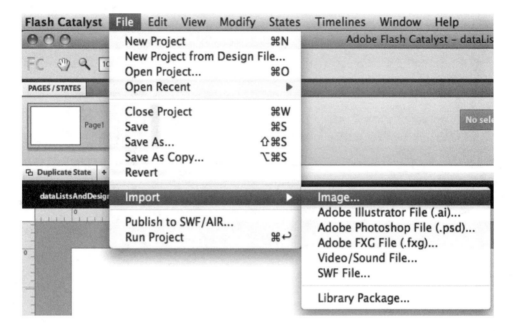

Figure 7-3. Importing images

Creating the Item to Be Repeated

Data List components are an effective way to manage the repeating items that are so common in interface design. Creating a Data List begins by creating a single item in the list. It can be simple, as with a single image, or sophisticated, involving several components. You then develop this single item, modifying the look of the item for its Over and Selected states, as well as adding animation.

For this example, the repeated item includes the book cover image and text boxes for the author name and release date. Although the author name and release date aren't visible until rollover, it's best to create your repeated item with all the pieces right away so they're included in the design-time data (which is covered later this chapter). If you miss an element, you can add it to the design-time data later. This example looks at how this is done.

At this point, the project has in its Library the six book covers you imported. To create the first repeated item, follow these steps:

1. Place the first of the six book covers onto the stage, as shown in Figure 7-4. To bring an image from the Library, select the file name and drag it onto the stage.

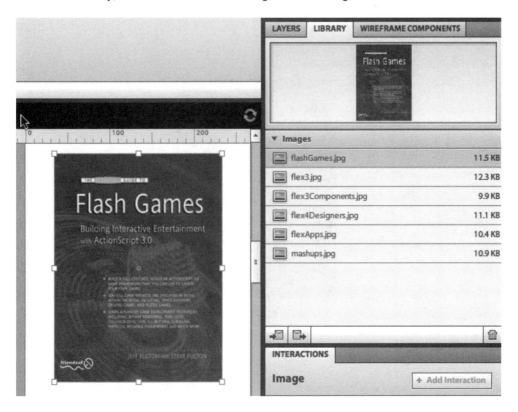

Figure 7-4. Placing the first book cover on the stage

2. The image is a bit large for a thumbnail and needs to be scaled down. (The original image is large because you use a larger version of the image later in the design.) Using the bounding-box handles, scale the image to be about 125 px wide by 165 px tall. Holding the Shift button as you scale the image maintains the aspect ratio, preventing it from distorting. You can also change the scale by entering the size of the image into the Properties panel.

Next, you need to add the other elements that make up the repeated item. For this design, you want to display the author name and release date when the user rolls over the cover. It's easiest to create at the start all the elements that go into the repeated item, although it's possible to add elements afterward.

3. Using the Text tool, add the text for the author name and release date, as shown in Figure 7-5. Because the content of the author name and release date text areas change for each author, draw the text area the width of the image, and set the alignment to Center (as opposed to creating it as point text).

Figure 7-5. The cover image with text areas for the author name and release date

Converting an Item into a Data List

You now have the all the elements for your repeated item. The next steps involve making these into a data list and then defining which items to repeat in the design-time data. This process is largely guided by the Heads-Up Display (HUD):

4. Select all three items that you've created. Using the HUD, convert them into a Data List, as shown in Figure 7-6.

Figure 7-6. converting elements to a Data List

Because a Data List is a more complicated component than, say, a button, Catalyst needs a bit more information to know how to properly convert the visual assets into a data list. The HUD attempts to guide you through this process. Specifically, Catalyst needs you to identify which of the items are repeated.

In the HUD, click Edit Parts, as shown in Figure 7-7. Doing so brings you inside the Data List component.

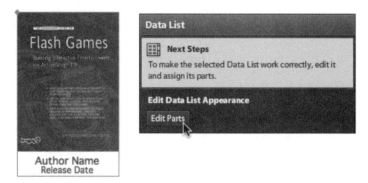

Figure 7-7. Editing the Data List parts

5. Because you want to repeat all the items, select them all. In the HUD, select Choose Part ➤ Repeated Item (Required), as shown in Figure 7-8.

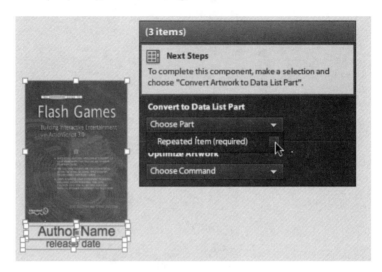

Figure 7-8. Defining an image and two text boxes as the repeated items in the Data List

The book cover and two text areas are now repeated to create a functioning Data List. The next steps are modifying the look of the Data List and then changing its design-time data.

Let's take a minute and look at what you've created. By default, the Data List created five identical repeated items and placed them in a vertical alignment. Your design should currently look similar to Figure 7-9: you can see three copies of the book cover and text that you created. Only these three are visible because the bounding box of the Data List cuts off the other two.

Figure 7-9. Default layout of the Data List

The Data List has also created two states, Normal and Disabled, as shown in Figure 7-10.

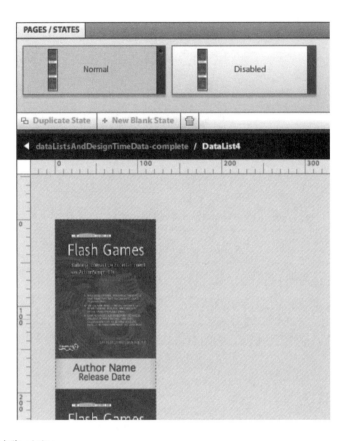

Figure 7-10. Data List's states

These two states affect how the Data List appears overall when it's in its Normal and Disabled settings. As you see later this chapter, the Data List has also created nested states that let you affect the rollover and selected setting for the repeated items.

Looking through the Properties panel for the Data List, shown in Figure 7-11, gives you a good indication what kinds of modifications are possible for this component. The most important settings are the Layout properties.

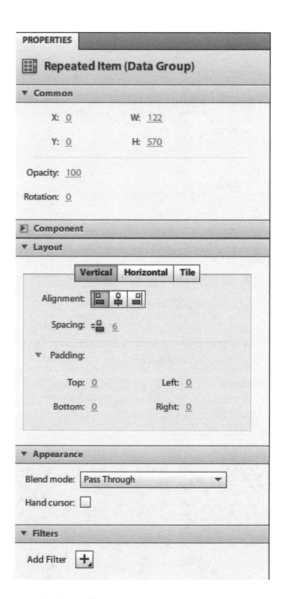

Figure 7-11. Properties panel for the Data List

You can control the Data List's layout by defining it as Vertical, Horizontal, or Tile. This design uses a horizontal layout; you add a scrollbar later. Because each repeated item in the design has the same height, the alignment settings have no impact. You can also change the spacing between the items. For this design, a 10 px space between the items works well:

6. Set the Data List to a Horizontal layout, and set the Spacing to be 10, as shown in Figure 7-12.

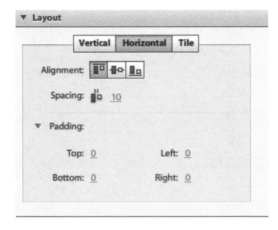

Figure 7-12. Layout properties for the Data List

At first, it appears that only one instance of the repeated item remains, because the bounding box doesn't automatically change with the bounding box of the Data List. You must do this manually:

7. Adjust the Data List's bounding box by dragging the handle, as shown in Figure 7-13. Note that it doesn't need to show all the items. You add a horizontal scrollbar later, so you can have items be outside the bounding box. Notice that the change in the layout only affects the Normal state—the Disabled state remains vertically aligned.

Figure 7-13. Data List with a horizontal layout and resized bounding box

8. To have the same layout and bounding box for the Normal and Disabled states, select the Data List in the Normal state and select Make Same in All Other States in the HUD, as shown in Figure 7-14.

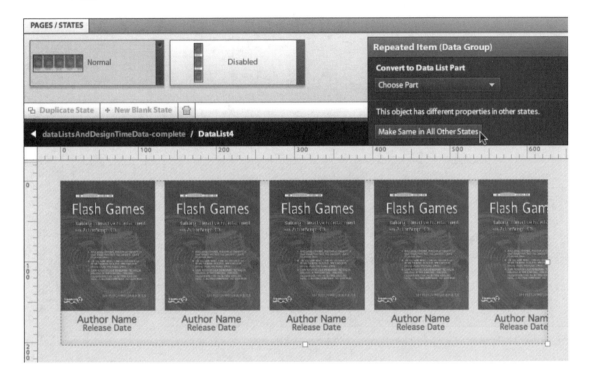

Figure 7-14. Making the Data List consistent across states

Creating Transitions on the Repeated Item

In addition to the Normal and Disabled states of the Data List as a whole, a Data List also creates a set of three states to control the appearance of the selected item. These states are called Normal, Over, and Selected. Just as you've seen with the states in of a button in previous chapters, these states affect how the repeated item appears based on user interaction. Unlike buttons, these states also automatically add an Item Highlight Rectangle that creates an automatic difference between the states.

Follow these steps:

1. To change the states for the repeated items, double-click one of them. This brings you into one repeated item and makes the others disappear temporarily. It doesn't matter which of the repeated items you double-click, because any changes to the states of one are included in all. The states at the beginning are the same with the exception of Item Highlight Rectangle.

Figure 7-15 shows the Item Highlight Rectangle on the stage and in the Layers panel. By default, this is a blue rectangle that is transparent in the Normal state, has a 30% opacity on the Over state, and has 50% opacity on the Selected state. This gives an automatic, if generic, highlighting to the Data List. You can test what this looks like in the browser by running the project (File ➤ Run Project).

Figure 7-15. Item Highlight Rectangle

As you can see in Figure 7-15, the Item Highlight Rectangle is placed on top of the image and text you created. This makes the image and text look washed out in your design. You can either remove the Item Highlight Rectangle completely by deleting it in the Layers panel (see Figure 7-16) or drag it below the other layers so the highlighting still exists but is behind the other elements.

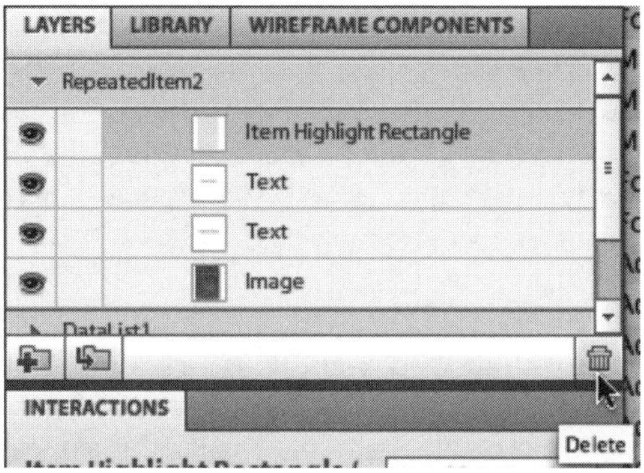

Figure 7-16. Deleting the Item Highlight Rectangle

2. For this example, move the Item Highlight Rectangle below the other elements so the highlighting remains but doesn't affect the clarity of the image (see Figure 7-17).

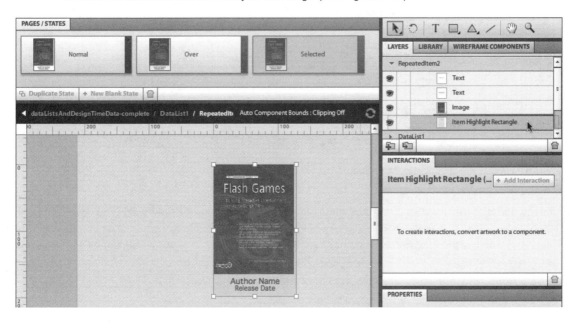

Figure 7-17. Dragging the Item Highlight Rectangle below the image and text

This design has the author name and release date move into position from behind the image on rollover and gives the image a drop shadow when selected. And because this is Catalyst, you animate between them.

The method of creating transitions for a repeated item follows the same process you saw in Chapter 4 and can include the same kinds of animation. As you saw in that chapter, you can do some complex animations with Catalyst. Because this chapter is more about working with Data Lists and design-time data, the animations are simple. Begin with the Normal state:

3. In the Normal state, the author name and release date are behind the image (so they can move into position in the Over state) Move the author name and release date text so that they're behind the image, as shown in Figure 7-18.

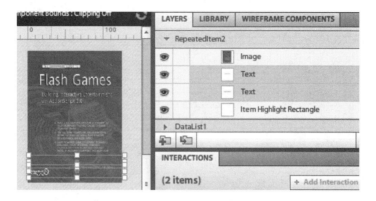

Figure 7-18. Moving the text behind the image in the Normal state

Nothing needs to be changed in the Over state, because it should look the way it did when you created it. The Selected state for a repeated item defines how the item looks after the user clicks that item. In a Data List, the last item clicked stays selected. To make it more obvious to the user which item is selected, you can affect the appearance of the Selected state:

    4.   In the Selected state, add a drop shadow effect to the image. To do so, add a Drop Shadow filter in the Properties panel, as shown in Figure 7-19.

Figure 7-19. Adding a Drop Shadow filter to the image in the Selected state

5. You can animate the transitions between states the same way you explored in Chapter 4. Smooth the transitions between the state changes in the Timelines panel, selecting all state transitions and clicking Smooth Transitions as shown in Figure 7-20. Doing so animates the movement of the text and changes the alpha of the Item Highlighting Rectangle, but not the Drop Shadow filter.

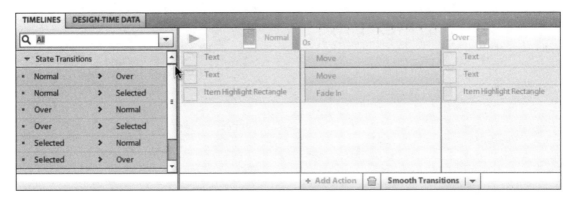

Figure 7-20. Smoothing the state transitions

Now is a good time to test your project to see how things are working (File ➤ Run Project). So far, the project involves five exact copies of the repeated item. When the user rolls over one of the book covers, the author name and release date appear from below the image. When the user clicks one of the items, a drop shadow is added, and that item remains selected until another repeated item is clicked.

This gives you an impression of what the final experience could be, but using identical images and text for each repeated item limits this. To get closer to the final experience of the site, you need different content in each of the repeated items. This is where design-time data comes in.

Using Design-Time Data

Design-time data is sample data that you can work with during the design phase in place of live data. Catalyst makes it very simple to change identical repeated items into a set of repeated items that better represents what the final project will look like while maintaining the behavior and animations you created for the first repeated item. It does this by changing the underlying data of the repeated item. For example, it changes the content of the text areas and the image, but the animations, drop shadows, and so on remain.

You can see this data on the Design-Time Data panel next to the Timelines panel. This data is structured the same way it would be if it was being brought in from an outside source. Figure 7-21 shows that the underlying data for the Data List is currently identical for each repeated item.

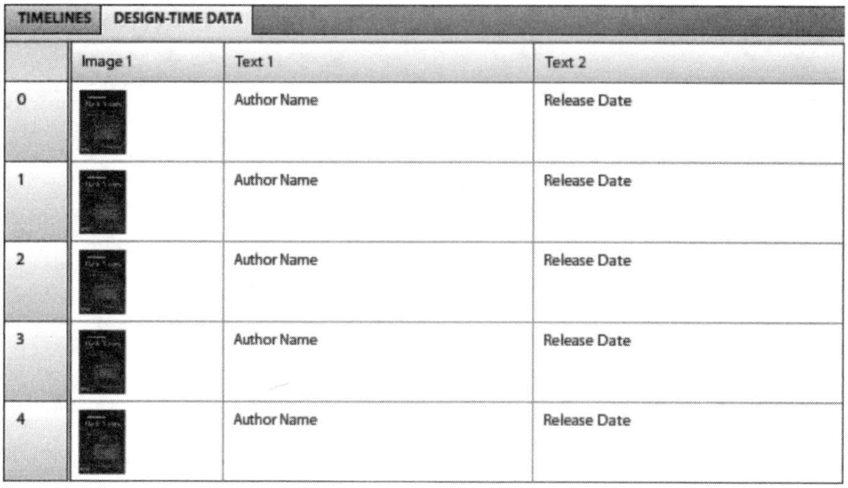
TIMELINES
DESIGN-TIME DATA
Image 1
Text 1
Text 2
0
Author Name
Release Date
1
Author Name
Release Date
2
Author Name
Release Date
3
Author Name
Release Date
4
Author Name
Release Date

Figure 7-21. Design-time data before modifications

To change the content for a given item, click it in the Design-Time Data panel; you're then presented with the most appropriate method of changing that kind of data. For images, this takes the form of a dialog box that lists the images in the Library and gives you the ability to import more (see Figure 7-22). Selecting a different book cover image from this list replaces the original image. The new image maintains the animations and filters of the original image and also fills the same bounding box. This means the image scales to fit the space that exists for the original image.

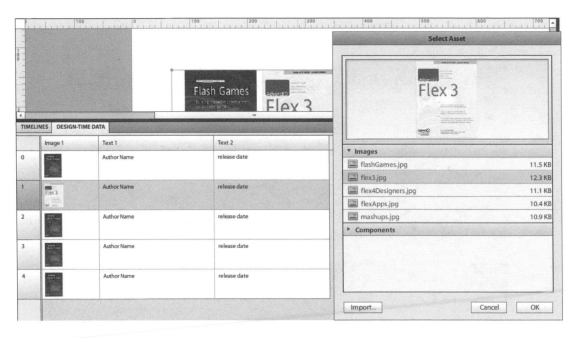

Figure 7-22. Select Asset dialog box in which you can change an image in the design-time data

Follow these steps:

1. Use the Select Asset dialog box to change the images to different images than those you previously imported.

Selecting a text area allows you to directly modify the text in it, as shown in Figure 7-23.

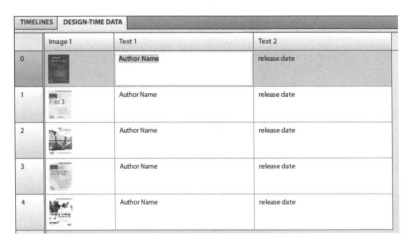

Figure 7-23. Changing text in the design-time data

2. Change the content Author Name and Release Date text areas by clicking each and entering new data (see Figure 7-24).

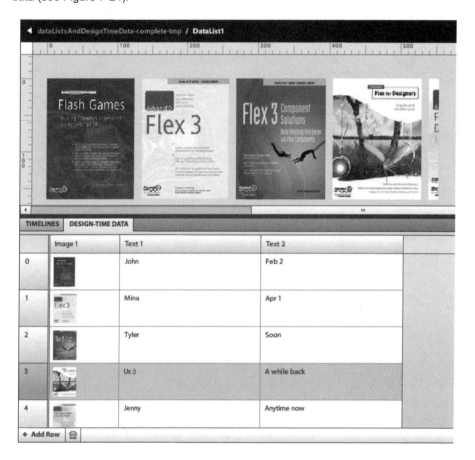

Figure 7-24. Changing text in the design-time data

You can see from how quickly you can change the content that after you create the structure and animations of a Data List, it's very easy to modify. It's also easy to add repeated items to the Data List. If you want to add another book to this Data List, all you need to do is add a row to the design-time data:

3. Add a repeated item by clicking the Add Row button at lower left in the Design-Time Data panel, as shown in Figure 7-25.

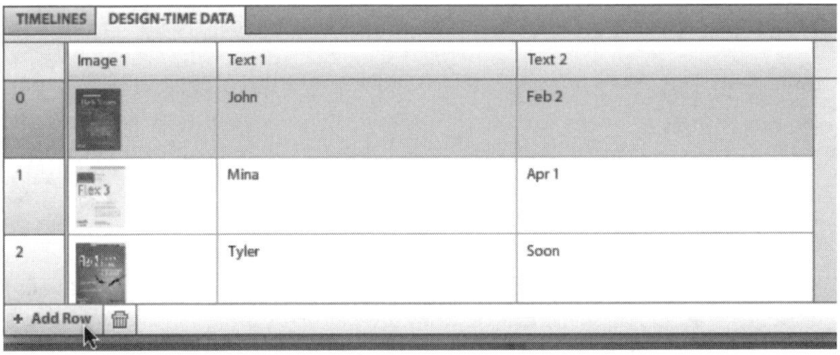

Figure 7-25. Adding a row to the design-time data

This creates a duplicate of the selected row that you can then modify. The new item also has all the animations and behaviors of the repeated item. This technique can serve as a quick method of working with recurring items in a design, especially if you have a large number of recurring items. But the biggest benefit comes later in the production process when the developer begins to work with the file. If you created each repeating item on its own—a button, for example—the developer would essentially have to re-create your layout and animations using live data.

But because the design-time data is structured the same as live data, the developer can swap the data. To see this, look at the code that was created for the Data List. As previously mentioned, all the work Catalyst does is captured in the form of MXML a markup language that developers can easily manipulate in Flash Builder. Figure 7-26 shows the design-time data for the Data List you just created.

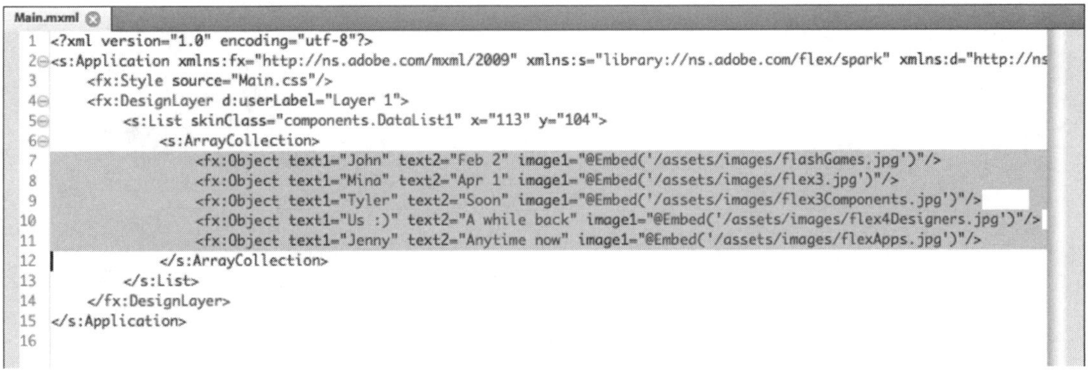

```
Main.mxml
 1  <?xml version="1.0" encoding="utf-8"?>
 2  <s:Application xmlns:fx="http://ns.adobe.com/mxml/2009" xmlns:s="library://ns.adobe.com/flex/spark" xmlns:d="http://ns
 3      <fx:Style source="Main.css"/>
 4      <fx:DesignLayer d:userLabel="Layer 1">
 5          <s:List skinClass="components.DataList1" x="113" y="104">
 6              <s:ArrayCollection>
 7                  <fx:Object text1="John" text2="Feb 2" image1="@Embed('/assets/images/flashGames.jpg')"/>
 8                  <fx:Object text1="Mina" text2="Apr 1" image1="@Embed('/assets/images/flex3.jpg')"/>
 9                  <fx:Object text1="Tyler" text2="Soon" image1="@Embed('/assets/images/flex3Components.jpg')"/>
10                  <fx:Object text1="Us :)" text2="A while back" image1="@Embed('/assets/images/flex4Designers.jpg')"/>
11                  <fx:Object text1="Jenny" text2="Anytime now" image1="@Embed('/assets/images/flexApps.jpg')"/>
12              </s:ArrayCollection>
13          </s:List>
14      </fx:DesignLayer>
15  </s:Application>
16
```

Figure 7-26. Code view of the design-time data

The highlighted parts of the code can be easily substituted by a repeater that enters live data from a database. The behaviors and animations you created are maintained exactly as they were in Catalyst.

Adding a Horizontal Scrollbar

With repeating items, you may find yourself in a situation where there are too many items for the space available. Usually, the answer to this kind of problem is the addition of a scrollbar. Adding one to a Data List is surprisingly straightforward: it involves placing a scrollbar inside the Data List, aligning it, and sizing it.

Here are the steps:

1. Double-click the component to enter it. In the Normal state, drag a horizontal scrollbar below the repeated items from the Wireframe Components panel (see Figure 7-27). You using a wireframe component here, but a custom-built one would work just as well.

Figure 7-27. Adding a scrollbar inside a Data List

2. Scale the scrollbar as shown in Figure 7-28, using the bounding-box handles. It's positioned a bit low so there is room for the rollover text.

Figure 7-28. Scrollbar after being scaled and positioned

And that, surprisingly, is all you need to do to add a scrollbar to a Data List. Run the project (File ➤ Run Project) to see it in action. The scrollbar thumb and the distance it moves along the track are automatically sized as appropriate.

Conclusion

This chapter looked at how you can repeat a single item in a design using the Data List component to create a set. By changing the repeated item, you can create a wide variety of interface elements, from galleries to blog posts to calendars. Each of them is similar because they're all created through the repetition of a singular item.

You also looked at how to use design-time data to substitute for live data during the design phase, allowing for the project to appear closer to the final product without a developer getting involved.

The next chapter looks at how to bring in video, audio, and SWFs to create a more compelling experience for the user.

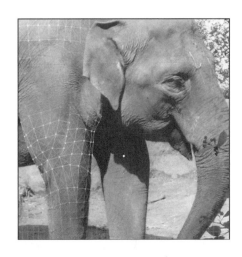

Chapter 8

SWFs, Video, and Audio

What we'll cover in this chapter:

- Controlling SWFs
- Using sound effects
- Controlling video

Files used in this chapter:

- `weatherApp-start.fxp`
- `weatherApp-complete.fxp`
- `weather.swf`
- Folder: `weatherIcons`

Although Catalyst has the ability to create some fairly sophisticated animated transitions, Flash's use of the timeline, guide paths, and scripted animation make it a much more powerful and flexible animation tool. Thankfully, as part of the Flash platform, Catalyst works very efficiently with files created in Flash. This allows you to create elaborate animations that involve numerous elements in Flash and then bring them into Catalyst. This lets you not only use the advanced animation tools of Flash, but also use your existing Flash skills in your Catalyst projects.

It's also possible to control Flash SWFs in Catalyst by using the Play, Stop and Go to Frame and Play, and Go to Frame and Stop action commands. These let you use user interactions to control which part of the SWF is playing. In this chapter's example, you bring in two sets of SWF files that represent two different ways of using files created with Flash in Catalyst projects. First, you use animated icons: simple files with looping animation that don't need to be controlled by user interaction. Second, you add an animated background that has greater complexity and is controlled by the user's actions.

Along with importing and controlling SWFs, this chapter looks at working with video and audio. You can bring in and control video and audio files similarly to the way you control SWFs via action sequences. (This is the main reason these topics appear in the same chapter.) They also add significant life to an interactive project. You looked quickly at adding audio in the project for the singer Amanda Moscar in Chapter 2, where you played an audio clip. This time, you use audio to add to the interaction design in the form of audio feedback for rollovers and clicks. The chapter looks at the audio elements included in Catalyst as well as including video in a Catalyst project.

A Quick Look at the Project

To look at the use of SWFs, audio, and video, you create a weather app prototype showing weather information for multiple cities. The weather conditions are presented through the use of animated icons created in Flash. A more elaborate Flash animation serves as the background, as shown in Figure 8-1. Changes in the background animation are triggered by the user rolling over one of the icons. Because this is a prototype, all the information is static. The goal of this prototype is to give the impression of what the final application will feel like rather than to create a functioning application that uses real data.

Figure 8-1. First state of the weather app

Clicking one of the cities transitions to the second state, which plays a traffic video for that city, as shown in Figure 8-2. This second state gives you an opportunity to play with Catalyst's video controls. You can see this prototype working at `http://greggoralski.com/weatherApp`.

Figure 8-2. Second state of the weather app

To stay focused on the main purpose of the chapter—working with SWFs, video, and audio—much of the grunt work of building this app has been done for you. All the animations in the SWFs have been created, because this book assumes you either know Flash or work with an animator who does. You can find these SWFs on the book's download page at `www.friendsofed.com`. They include a set of four animated weather icons (`sunny.swf`, `rain.swf`, `cloud.swf`, and `lightning.swf`) as well as the background animation (`weather.swf`), as shown in Figure 8-3. The FLA file for `weather.swf` is also included because it's useful to see the structure of the original file, in order to see how it's being animated.

Figure 8-3. Files included in this chapter's example

Along with the SWFs, this project has a Catalyst file to get you started more quickly; it's named `weatherApp-start.fxp`. The completed file is named `weatherApp-complete.fxp`.

Begin by opening `weatherApp-start.fxp`, which has all the elements for the weather app prototype except the SWFs, video, audio, and interactions. The first state (cities) includes the static text *Current* and 28°, and a Data List with four cites and their temperatures (see Figure 8-4). This Data List was created in the same way you created Data Lists in the previous chapter.

Figure 8-4. Cities state of `weatherApp-start.fxp`

Adding Simple Animation SWFs

The first thing you want to do in this project is import the animated icons that are provided with the chapter. You import SWFs using a method similar to that you use to import images. You don't need to do anything in particular to the SWFs to prepare them for use in Catalyst; SWFs with AS2 or AS3 will work fine.

Follow these steps:

1. In weatherApp-start.fxp, import the set of SWFs in the weatherIcons folder. To import a SWF, select File ➤ Import ➤ SWF File in the main menu (see Figure 8-5). You can also import all the SWF files at once, as shown in Figure 8-6.

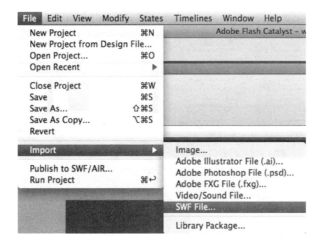

Figure 8-5. Importing SWF files

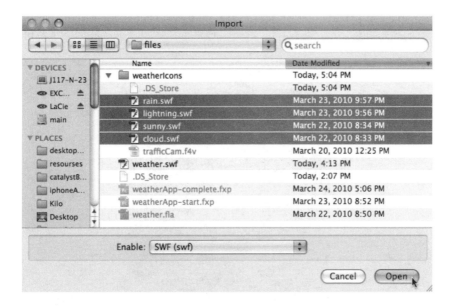

Figure 8-6. Selecting SWFs to import

As with images, if you import a single SWF, it's included in the Library, and an instance of it is automatically placed on the stage. But if multiple SWFs are imported together, they're included in the Library without an instance being placed on the stage. You can see the four SWFs in the Library, as shown in Figure 8-7. The SWFs are placed in the Images section of the Library because Catalyst treats SWFs in much the same way it does images.

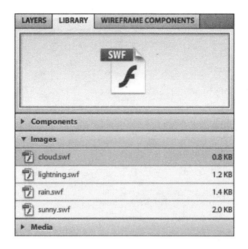

Figure 8-7. SWF files in the Library

2. Just like images, to add the SWF files to the stage, you select the file name in the Library and drag onto the stage. Drag these SWFs onto the stage, and position them on top of the Data List as shown in Figure 8-8. The SWFs also need to be scaled to better fit with the design; to do this, use the bounding-box handles.

Figure 8-8. Placing SWF files on the stage

Notice that when you scale the SWF, it maintains its aspect ratio and doesn't distort that actual SWF. This is because the scaling changes the bounding box in which the SWF is imported.

Test the project (File ➤ Run Project) to see how the SWFs respond in the Catalyst project. The SWFs automatically begin playing and continue to loop unless something stops them. You can stop the SWFs either by an interaction triggering an action sequence (as you see in a moment) or by using a stop command in the SWF.

Looking at the Layers panel, you can see that each SWF has been added to a layer named SWF Asset (see Figure 8-9).

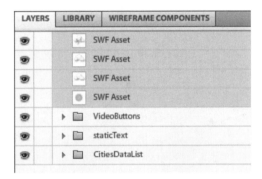

Figure 8-9. SWFs in the Layers panel

This is hardly a useful name; and as discussed in Chapter 6, naming is of great importance in helping the developers understand your files down the production path. Rename the SWFs **sunIcon**, **cloudIcon**, **rainIcon**, and **lightningIcon**. To keep things neat, you can also place them in their own folder (see Figure 8-10) called **weatherIcons**.

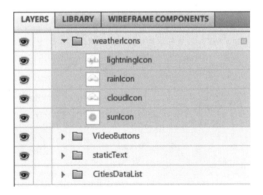

Figure 8-10. Renaming the SWF files

A quick look, for the courageous, at the code created when you placed the SWFs on the stage gives you more insight into how Catalyst handles SWFs (see Figure 8-11). To see it in Catalyst, switch from design to code view (upper right of the stage), and scroll down. This piece of code shows that the SWF file isn't actually brought into Catalyst but rather is copied to a folder in the project (assets/images/) and linked to from there. This means that if you need to change the animated icon in the future, you don't have to reimport the SWF and recreate the placement/scaling; rather, you can replace the SWF in the assets/images/ folder.

```
<fx:DesignLayer d:userLabel="weatherIcons">
    <fclib:SWFController height="52" id="swfcontroller1" includeIn="cities" loadForCompatibility="true" source="assets/images/sunny.swf" d:userLabel="sunIcon" width="50" x="175" y="203"/>
    <fclib:SWFController height="48" id="swfcontroller2" includeIn="cities" loadForCompatibility="true" source="assets/images/cloud.swf" d:userLabel="cloudIcon" width="49" x="176" y="258"/>
    <fclib:SWFController height="51" id="swfcontroller3" includeIn="cities" loadForCompatibility="true" source="assets/images/rain.swf" d:userLabel="rainIcon" width="51" x="175" y="305"/>
    <fclib:SWFController height="55" id="swfcontroller4" includeIn="cities" loadForCompatibility="true" source="assets/images/lightning.swf" d:userLabel="lightningIcon" width="55" x="173" y="351"/>
</fx:DesignLayer>
```

Figure 8-11. MXML code created when the weather icons were placed on the stage

Controlling SWFs

Because the weather icons don't need to be controlled by user interaction but are instead allowed to loop, they're easy to deal with, and you don't have to be concerned about how they're constructed. This is the FLAs aren't included for those files—it's enough for you to know that they play their animations.

But if you want to gain more control over a SWF and have the user interaction control it, you need to better understand how the SWF was built. Catalyst gives you control over a SWF file through the commands Play, Stop, Go to Frame and Play, and Go to Frame and Stop. Play and Stop commands control the SWF from the current frame it's in, whereas Go to Frame and Play and Go to Frame and Stop allow you to select the frame number to begin at in the SWF's main timeline.

This control is limited, because you can't use frame labels, control nested movie clips, or pass variable information. But, creatively used, it's generally enough to let you create sophisticated prototypes. More advanced manipulation of a SWF needs to take place in Flash Builder.

In this section of the example, you bring in a background animation that animates when the user rolls over one of the weather icons. To better understand this, it may be useful to look at the completed example, http://greggoralski.com/weatherApp.

Notice that as you roll over a weather icon, the background animates and shows a photorealistic representation of the weather on the icon. Let's first look at the Flash file that contains the animation:

1. Open weather.fla in Adobe Flash. This file is structured as one long animation in the main timeline, because the main timeline is the only part of a SWF that you can control in Catalyst. Figure 8-12 shows the structure of the Flash file.

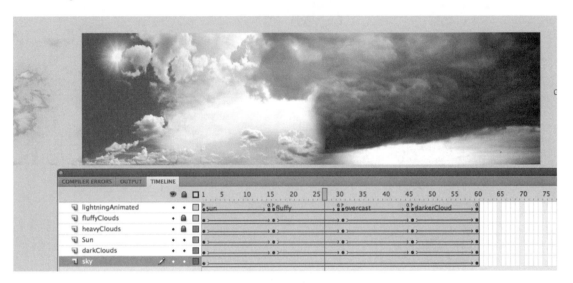

Figure 8-12. The weather.fla file in the main timeline

This Flash file has the same stage size as the Catalyst file and is made up of a series of movie clips representing the weather conditions of the weather icons. Each weather condition has an animation of 15 frames followed by a stop() command. The stop() is the only code in this file. There is no real limit to how complicated and layered the animation is in the main timeline; it can also include nested animations. The lightning animation, for example, is nested in a movie clip. Continue as follows:

2. Import weather.swf into the Catalyst project using the same technique you used to import the weather icons (File ➤ Import SWF File). Because you're importing only one SWF this time, an instance of it is placed on the stage in the top layer automatically (see Figure 8-13). This places it on top of all the existing assets.

3. Drag the layer with this SWF to the bottom in the Layers panel, and rename it backgroundAnimation, as shown in Figure 8-14.

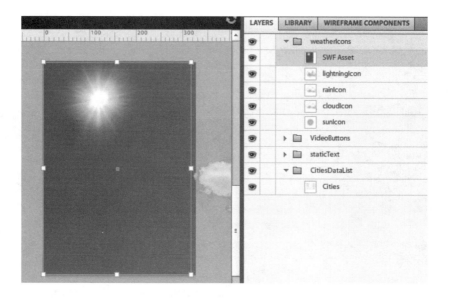

Figure 8-13. Imported SWF on the top layer

Figure 8-14. SWF renamed and placed at the bottom of the Layers list

You control a SWF using the Add Action button in the Timelines panel that you first saw in Chapter 5. The Add Action button gives you access to a variety of controls for SWFs, audio, and video and can be triggered by either a state change or an action sequence. Action sequences differ from state changes because they're series of actions in the current state. Because it's more direct and efficient in this case to use action sequences rather than create a new state for each weather condition, you use action sequences for this example.

To create an action sequence, you begin by creating the interaction that triggers the sequence. In the case, the interaction is the user rolling over the weather icons:

4. Select the first weather icon, sunIcon. In the Interactions panel, click Add Interaction. In the resulting dialog box, set the Interaction to be On Roll Over ➤ Play Action Sequence (see Figure 8-15). This creates a space for the action sequence in the Timelines panel, to which you can add actions (see Figure 8-16).

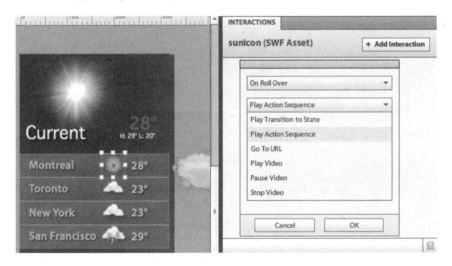

Figure 8-15. Interaction for sunIcon

Figure 8-16. Action sequence in the Timelines panel

5. The action sequence is ready to have actions added to it. To do so, with the action sequence selected in the Timelines panel, select the object that is affected by the action (in this case, backgroundAnimation) and click Add Action (see Figure 8-17).

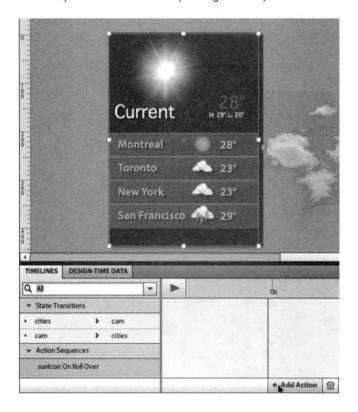

Figure 8-17. Adding an action to backgroundAnimation in the action sequence

The Add Action command gives you a variety of options for the control of SWFs, video, and audio. To control SWFs, as mentioned earlier, the options are Play, Stop, Go to Frame and Play, and Go to Frame and Stop. In this example, each weather icon triggers a Go to Frame and Play action. Specifically, each icon goes to the frame in which its associated animation exists in the weather.swf file (these are staggered every 15 frames):

6. Add the action SWF Control ➤ Go to Frame and Play in this action sequence, as shown in Figure 8-18.

Figure 8-18. Adding the Go to Frame and Play action to the action sequence

After you add the action, you can control the frame at which to begin the animation via the Properties panel for the action. For the animation associated with sunIcon, the animation begins at frame number 1:

7. Set the start frame for the action to 1 in the Properties panel (see Figure 8-19).

Figure 8-19. Setting the start frame for the action in the Properties panel

Test the effect of this action sequence by running the project (File ➤ Run Project). Notice that as you roll over sunIcon, a background animation bringing in a few clouds plays in the background. The animations for cloudIcon, rainIcon, and lightningIcon are more dramatic. To create the action sequences that trigger these animations, follow the same process you did for the first of the weather icons:

8. Select the weather icon for which you want to create an action sequence, and click Add Interaction. In the Timelines panel, select the action sequence. On the stage, select backgroundAnimation, add the action SWF Control ➤ Go to Frame and Play, and define the start frame.

Each icon starts the animation on a different frame: cloudIcon's start frame is 16, rainIcon's start frame is 31, and lightningIcon's start frame is 46. These numbers are based on where in the main timeline of the Flash file the animations begin. Because of this, it's important that you have access to original Flash file when working with a more complicated animation. Where the animation stops is controlled by the stop commands in the Flash file.

Adding Audio Effects

You also use the Add Action command to trigger audio effects in a project. You've looked at how the Add Action command adds actions to an action sequence, but you can also use it to add actions to a state transition. To see this, you can add a sound effect to the transition from the cities state you've been working in to the cam state that holds the video example. The cam state has been created for you in this project, so all you need to do is add the audio effect to the transition and trigger the transition through an interaction. Let's add the audio effect first:

1. Select the cities ➤ cam state transition in the Timelines panel, and click Add Action (see Figure 8-20).

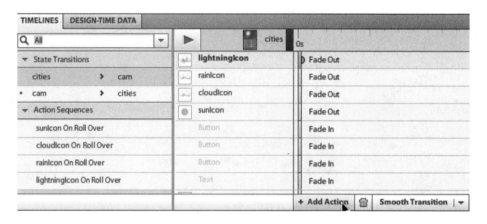

Figure 8-20. Selecting a transition in the Timelines panel

2. In the Add Action command, select Sound Effect (see Figure 8-21).

Figure 8-21. Choosing Sound Effect in the Add Action options

This option brings up an Import dialog box that allows you to select an audio asset to be played at this transition (see Figure 8-22). This dialog box shows all the audio files in your Library. If you want to bring in a custom MP3 to include, you can choose File ➤ Import Sound/Video File as you did in Chapter 2. Any imported audio files appear in this dialog box. You can also import files via the Import button in this dialog box. By default, clicking the Import button in this dialog box opens the folder of audio files that are included with Catalyst (see Figure 8-22). This is a collection of frequently used interaction audio effects:

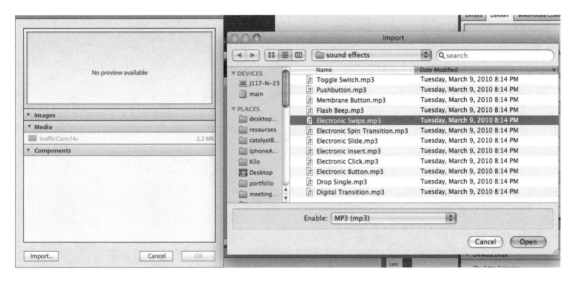

Figure 8-22. Selecting a sound effect

3. Select Import ➤ Electricon Swipe.mp3, and click Open. Doing so imports the audio file into the Library. Click OK to add this audio to the transition (see Figure 8-23).

The sound file is added to the transition in the Timelines panel (see Figure 8-24). By default, the sound file is given 1 second, which is generally plenty of time. You can lengthen or shorten it by changing the Length property of the sound effect in the Properties panel.

Figure 8-23. Adding a sound effect to a transition

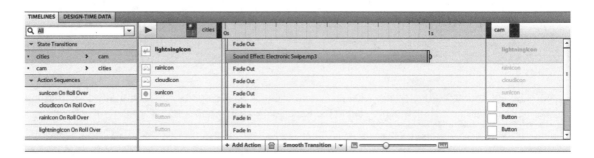

Figure 8-24. Sound effect in the Timelines panel

4. While you're here, click the Smooth Transitions button to make the transition between the cities state and the cam state animate.

5. To add sound effects to the rollover action sequences you created for the weather icons, follow a similar process—with the exception that, instead of adding an action on a transition, you add it to the action sequence associated with the weather icon, as shown in Figure 8-25.

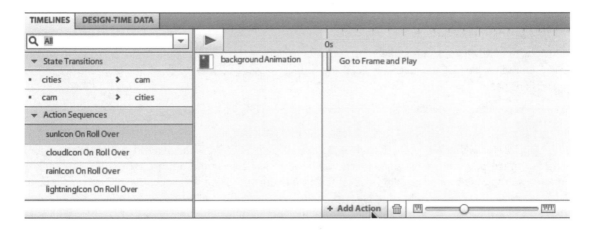

Figure 8-25. Adding a sound effect to an action sequence

To hear the sound effect on the transition, you need to have some sort of interaction trigger the transition. The most appropriate way to do this in this example is to have the Data List (the one that holds the name of each city and its temperature) trigger the transition to the cam state:

6. In the cities state, select the Data List. In the Interactions panel, add the interaction On Select ➤ Play Transition to State ➤ cam, as shown in Figure 8-26.

Figure 8-26. Interaction settings for the Data List

Adding Video

Adding video follows the same straightforward process you've seen for adding the SWFs. You can largely follow the same kind of process to control the video, except you can also add actions directly in the Interactions panel.

To bring video into the cam state, select this state, and then follow these steps:

1. In the cam state, select Import ➤ Video/Sound File, and then select trafficCam.f4v from the files provided with this chapter. Doing so places an instance of the video in a Video Player component on the stage at its full size, which you need to scale to fit the design. By default, the scaling setting on the video in Catalyst is Letterbox and doesn't distort the video. Flash Catalyst supports .flv and .f4v files. Both of these are container formats that allow for video that is compressed using a variety of codecs including H.264 and On2 VP6.

2. Scale the video so it fits with the design, as shown in Figure 8-27.

Figure 8-27. Video scaled in the cam state

The controls along the bottom of the video are automatically added. These can take the form of the default wireframe skins, which are shown in Figure 8-27, or standard skins that appear similar to the video player in Flash. You can also remove the video controls by setting Video Controls to None. You do so in the Properties panel for the video. You can control the video using these controls or using actions, similar to how you control SWFs:

3. Select the video and in the Properties panel, select None in the Video Controls drop-down (see Figure 8-28).

Figure 8-28. Setting Video Controls to None

Looking over the Properties panel, you can see the kinds of changes that are possible for the video. You can change the opacity, rotation, and scale mode; you can also set the video to Auto Play (by default, the video pauses on the first frame), Loop, or Muted (see Figure 8-29).

To show how custom video controls work, the project has a series of buttons along the bottom of this state. The buttons are Play, Pause, and Stop; they're used to control the video. You can add an action to a video the same way you added the backgroundAnimation SWF, but you can also add it directly in the Interactions panel:

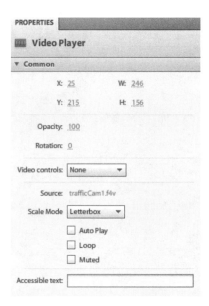

Figure 8-29. Video player properties

4. Select the Play button. In the Interactions panel, set the interaction to On Click ➤ Play Video (see Figure 8-30).

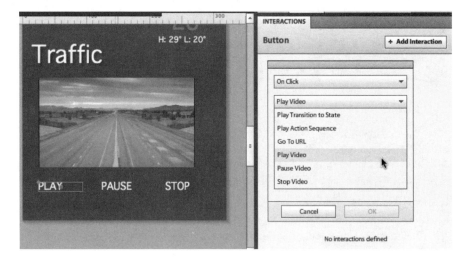

Figure 8-30. Setting the interaction to Play Video

You can use the same kind of direct method to pause and stop the video.

Conclusion

You can now run the project (File ➤ Run Project) to see how the prototype behaves. This example illustrates that you can quickly add SWFs, audio, and video to create a more compelling prototype with more sophisticated animation.

The next chapter looks at some of Catalyst's more advanced features, including custom components and library packages.

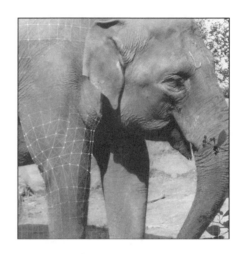

Chapter 9

Custom Components and Library Packages

What we'll cover in this chapter:

- Creating custom components

- Exporting library packages

Files used in this chapter:

- customComponent-start.fxp

- customComponent-complete.fxp

Catalyst comes with a variety of components that cover most interaction situations. These include components such as the button and the horizontal slider, and other components that are included in the wireframe component set and were used in Chapter 3. Inevitably, you stumble onto a situation where these default components aren't appropriate and you want to create a different sort of interaction. This is where custom/generic components come into play.

Custom/generic components are used primarily in two situations. The first of these is when you need to add interactions to an object that doesn't have them; this is the generic type of component. The second is more sophisticated and involves creating custom functionality for a component. You look at an example of this later in this chapter in the form of a custom navigation bar.

Creating a Generic Component

The simplest use of the custom/generic component adds interaction to an object that doesn't have it. This is most often the case with images that are used to trigger interactions. As you can see in Figure 9-1, you can't add interactions directly to an image.

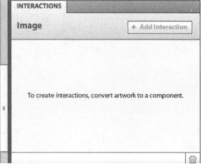

Figure 9-1. Image and Interactions panel

By converting the image into a custom/generic component, you can use the image to trigger state changes or action sequences (see Figure 9-2) the same way you use a button component.

Figure 9-2. Custom/Generic component and Interactions panel

To create a custom/generic component from an image or other kind of object, first select the image. Then, in the HUD, select Convert Artwork to Component ➤ Custom/Generic Component, as shown in Figure 9-3.

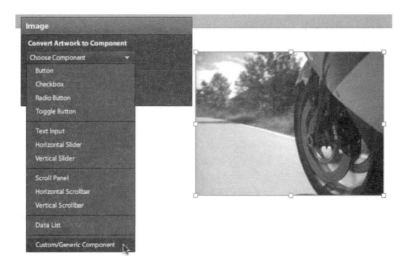

Figure 9-3. Converting an image to a custom/generic component

This places the image into a custom/generic component containing a single state (named state1 by default). The resulting component is very simple and doesn't have any unnecessary states or interactions (see Figure 9-4).

Figure 9-4. Simple custom/generic component

Creating a Custom Component

A custom component begins much the same way as a generic component, but then you add states and behaviors to create custom functionality. You can wrap a set of objects (images, text, or other components) into a single component and then add states in it. These states can then be changed through interactions to create the component's behavior. This allows you to create unique interactions and minimize the number of states in the main stage. As a result, the project is more manageable.

For example, this approach is particularly useful in animated menu systems. Such a menu system requires multiple states (for the animation), and it usually appears on multiple states/pages throughout the project. By wrapping a menu system in a custom component, you can create sophisticated animation across multiple states while keeping the menu as a single component on the stage.

The example in this chapter illustrates by creating a menu system that opens and closes based on user interaction; you can find the complete example at www.greggoralski.com/customComponent. The menu begins closed (see Figure 9-5) and opens when you click Menu + (see Figure 9-6).

Figure 9-5. Closed menu

Figure 9-6. Open menu

You can also select items when the menu is in its compressed state, as shown in Figure 9-7.

Figure 9-7. Menu open at contact

To create the menu system, you need four buttons (one for each menu item) and a toggle button, which is used to open and close the menu (see Figure 9-8).

Figure 9-8. Assets needed for the animated menu

These assets are included in the provided file `customMenu-start.fxp`. Follow these steps to create the menu:

1. Open the `customMenu-start.fxp` file in Catalyst, and look at the assets. The four main buttons—About, Works, Contact, and Blog—are all simple buttons. Menu + is a toggle button; it appears as Menu - in its selected state (see Figure 9-9), which indicates to the user that the button is used to open and close the menu.

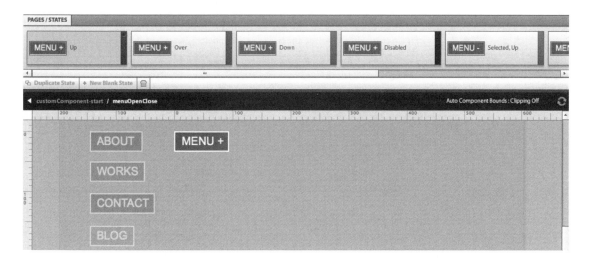

Figure 9-9. Menu + toggle button

2. You create a custom component much the same way as any other component. The difference is that instead of selecting one of the standard components in the HUD, you select Custom/Generic Component. Select all the buttons, and, in the HUD, select Convert Artwork to Component ➤ Custom/Generic Component, as shown in Figure 9-10. Doing so places all the assets into a custom component named CustomComponent1. (As you saw in Chapter 6, clear naming makes Catalyst projects much easier to manage through the development process.)

Figure 9-10. Converting the animated menu's assets into a custom/generic gomponent

3. In the Library panel, rename the component **Menu** (see Figure 9-11).

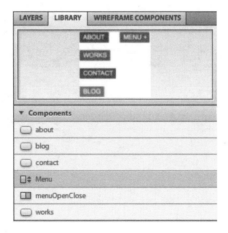

Figure 9-11. Renaming the custom component Menu

This new component contains all the assets of the menu but doesn't yet have any custom functionality. The custom functionality in this case consists of opening and closing the menu, along with the way the menu reveals the nested options on rollover.

To create this kind of functionality, you enter the custom component and, using the same techniques you use to create states in the main stage, add states that show how the component is to appear in various circumstances. Then, you create the interactions that reveal those states:

4. To enter the custom component, either double-click it or select Edit Custom Component Appearance ➤ State1 in the HUD (see Figure 9-12). The component contains a single state: State1. You can add more states to animate the menu.

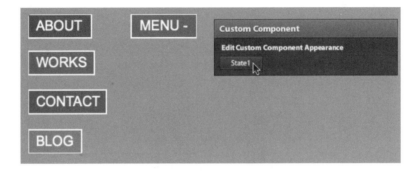

Figure 9-12. Entering the custom component

5. Change State1's name to **Open**. This state represents how the custom component appears when it's open.

6. Rearrange the buttons and the toggle button the way they should appear when the menu is open (see Figure 9-13). In the Properties panel, set the toggle button to be selected; this displays the toggle button as Menu -, indicating that clicking it will close the menu when the menu is open. With the Open state complete, you can now create the Closed state for the menu system.

Figure 9-13. Layout of the elements in the Open state

7. Click Duplicate State, as shown in Figure 9-14, and name the new state **Closed**.

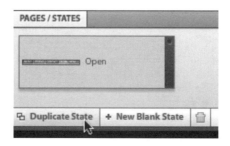

Figure 9-14. Duplicating the Open state

8. Modify the position of the buttons to represent the menu's Closed state, as shown in Figure 9-15. In the Properties panel, set the toggle button to be not selected; this displays the toggle button as Menu +.

Figure 9-15. Menu in the Closed state

You've now created the way you want the custom menu to appear when it's open and when it's closed. The menu also has additional functionality: when it's closed, clicking any of the hidden buttons expands that part of the menu, revealing the clicked button. Figure 9-16 shows how the menu appears when the Works button is rolled over. To give the menu this kind of functionality, you need to create a state that indicates how the menu appears when each button is rolled over:

Figure 9-16. Appearance of the menu when you roll over the Works button

9. For each button—About, Works, Contact, and Blog—duplicate the Closed state and adjust the layout so one button at a time is fully visible. For example, make the layout shown in Figure 9-16 into a state named **works**. The result is four new states, one for each button. Name each new state after the button that's visible in it, as shown in Figure 9-17.

Figure 9-17. States for the menu's four buttons

You've now created all the states for the custom component. You can think of this as having created the structure of the component; next, you breathe life into it by adding interactions.

Adding Interactions

The custom component has six states; Open, Closed, and a state for each of the four buttons. To control when each of these states is visible, you add interactions to the buttons using the same technique you used in Chapter 5.

Let's begin with the About button:

1. In the custom component, select the About button. In the Interactions panel, click Add Interaction. Doing so brings up the Interactions dialog box, where you can define the interaction for this part of the component. In this case, any time the About button is clicked, you want to transition to the state in which the menu is compressed but shows the About button (the state named about).

2. In the Interactions dialog box, set the interaction to be On Click ➤ Play Transition to State ➤ about, as shown in Figure 9-18.

3. Add similar interactions to the three remaining buttons (Works, Contact, and Blog) by repeating steps 1 and 2 for each.

The state in which you create these interactions doesn't matter, because the interactions for a component stay with the component in all of its states.

Also note that when there are other states on the main stage, they also appear as options to transition to. This allows a button in a custom component to affect not just the states in the component but also those outside of it. This project currently doesn't have a state in the main stage; but if it had one named newState, it would appear as shown in Figure 9-19.

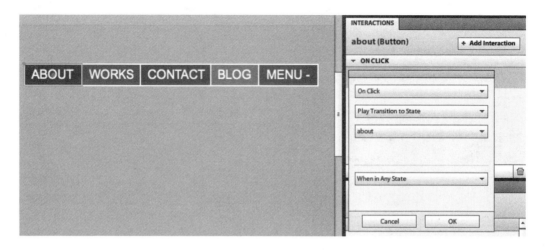

Figure 9-18. Adding an interaction to the About button

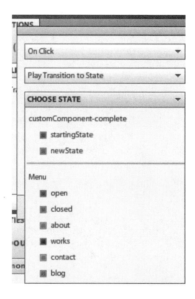

Figure 9-19. Interactions panel if multiple states exist on the main stage

Similarly, the states you create in the custom component are included in the states listed in the Interactions panel for components outside the custom component. This allows outside buttons to affect the states in the custom component.

The toggle button (named menuOpenClose) is slightly different, because it needs to both open and close the menu system:

4. For the toggle button, set the interaction to be On Click ➤ Play Transition to State ➤ open, as shown in Figure 9-20. This covers all the situations when you want the menu to open.

Figure 9-20. Interaction for the toggle button

5. There is only one situation in which you want clicking the toggle button to close the menu: when the menu is already open. Add a second interaction to the toggle button, set to On Click ➤ Play Transition to State ➤ closed ➤ When in open, as shown in Figure 9-21.

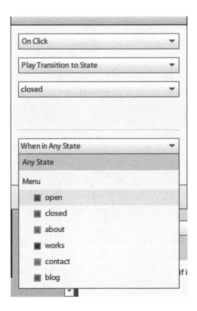

Figure 9-21. Second interaction for the toggle button

This interaction closes the menu system when the toggle button in clicked in the Open state. This works despite the second statement conflicting with the first, because the second command overrides the first. A single component in Catalyst can have multiple interactions, with interactions you create later overriding earlier interactions if there are conflicts. For example, the toggle button currently has two interactions, as shown in Figure 9-22. In this case, "Play Transition to closed if in open" comes after "Play Transition to open," overriding it. This example wouldn't work if the two interactions were reversed.

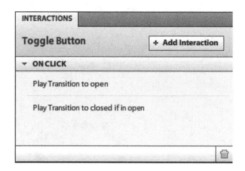

Figure 9-22. Interactions for the toggle button

6. As a final touch, set the menu to animate to the Close state when the application starts. To create this interaction, jump to the project's main stage, and click an empty area of the stage (doing so sets the application as the target of the Interactions panel). In the Interactions panel, set the interaction to On Application Start ➤ Play Transition to State ➤ closed, as shown in Figure 9-23.

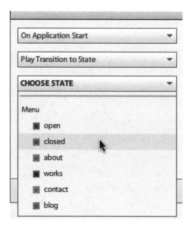

Figure 9-23. Interaction on application start

Adding Animation

To animate the menu, you need to smooth the transition between the states: in the Timelines panel, select all the transitions, and click Smooth Transitions (see Figure 9-24). Notice that because you now have six states, the list of possible transitions is rather long; but it's preferable to have them encapsulated in the custom component rather than have them add to the number of states on the main stage.

Figure 9-24. Smoothing the transitions between states

The menu system is now complete. Run the project to see it in action.

Library Packages

Having created the menu system, you may want to share this custom component across multiple Catalyst projects or Flash Builder directly. To do this, you export it as a Library package (FXPL). Library packages contain all the custom components, component skins, and supporting assets of a project but without the MXML file that defines the project's layout (the MXML is created in the background as you lay out your project on the main stage). Essentially, everything in your Library can be wrapped up and passed to multiple projects.

The Export Library Package button is at the bottom of the Library panel, as shown in Figure 2-25.

The Import Library Package button is directly to the left. Clicking it lets you open an FXPL file and import all the visual assets, skins, and custom components it contains.

Creating custom components is a useful technique because you can build a library of assets that you can use over and over again in multiple projects. Flash Catalyst can handle a large variety of projects and use cases, but sometimes the complexity of a project demands that you create an application in Flash Builder. In my experience, this happens the second you feel the need to add a custom micro-architecture: when you modify the code in Flash Builder, it's impossible for Flash Catalyst to account for the changes. Creating as much as possible of your application as separate, reusable components helps you save time skinning parts of the project. Even if you decide to create a project in Flash Builder, you can use Flash Catalyst to export components' Library packages and speed up your project.

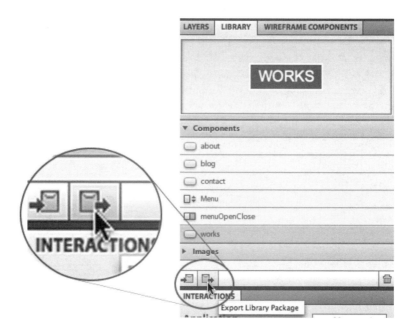

Figure 9-25. Import and Export Library Package buttons

Conclusion

With the example of the animated menu, you've seen how to go beyond the set of components that ships with Catalyst and create your own custom components. In most situations, the preexisting components work fine, and they're often faster because they come prebuilt. But it's useful to know that when you want a unique interaction, you can create it in Catalyst using custom components.

In the next chapter, you look at how you can take a project created in Catalyst into Flash Builder to connect it to live data and complete it. In most production processes, a dedicated developer handles the conversion of the Catalyst project into a completed site with live data; but understanding how this works gives you greater insight into how to build Catalyst projects so the process goes more smoothly.

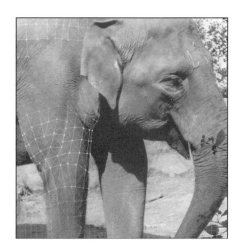

Chapter 10

Catalyst to Flex Builder

What we'll cover in this chapter:

- Creating a custom vertical scrollbar

- Importing Catalyst files into Flash Builder

- Connecting a Data List component to an XML file

Files used in this chapter:

- `wineJournal-start.fxp`

- `wineJournal-complete.fxp`

- `wineJournal-complete-withXML.fxp`

- `XMLAndImages.zip`

- `verticalScrollBar.ai`

One of the key advantages of Catalyst is that it separates the work done by interaction designers from the work done by developers. Interaction designers get to build in Catalyst using visual tools with design-time data and no coding, and developers can work from the same file in a much more code-friendly environment to connect it with a variety of data sources. This transition can often be difficult, largely due to the dramatically different ways each group works with the file.

This chapter looks at this transition by building out an application in Catalyst using static data and then connecting it with an outside data source in Flash Builder. The outside data source is a simple XML file, to keep the chapter focused on the transition rather than the data-handling capabilities of Flash Builder. The process you use, though, is very similar regardless of the data source. To complete this example, you need to bring it into Flash Builder. If you don't have Flash Builder installed, you can get a trial copy at `www.adobe.com/products/flashbuilder/`.

The example creates a Wine Journal app that is first built in Catalyst using static data. You then open the file in Flash Builder and use an XML file to populate the list and data that is shown when an item in the list is clicked. As an added bonus, you create a custom vertical scrollbar for the list. The completed file appears as shown in Figure 10-1 and can be seen working at `http://greggoralski.com/wineJournal`.

Figure 10-1. Finished application

In this application, the user first selects the kind of wine (see Figure 10-2). For the sake of speed, in this case you make only the Red button active, but you can use the same process to make the others function.

Figure 10-2. Artwork for the menu

This gives the user a list of wines to choose from (see Figure 10-3).

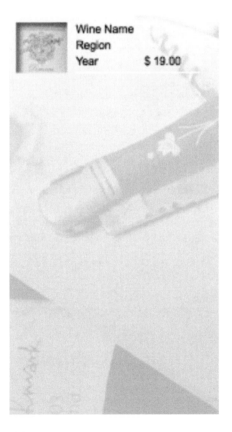

Figure 10-3. Artwork for the Data List

Selecting one of these brings up a detailed description and a larger image of the wine (see Figure 10-4).

Figure 10-4. Artwork for extended description

To save time and focus on the interesting bits, you start with a partially completed file called wineJournal-start.fxp. This file includes all the elements of the design as static objects before they're made into interactive components. In essence, this is a static comp of the design (see Figure 10-5). In Catalyst, you make it into an interactive comp, and in Flash Builder you connect it to an external data source.

Figure 10-5. Static elements of the provided design

Creating the Interaction in Catalyst

The first action the user performs in this site is selecting a kind of wine. For the sake of the example, you only create the functionality for the Red selection. Follow these steps:

1. Open the `wineJournal-start.fxp` file.

2. Select the *Red* text, and, in the HUD, convert it to a button as shown in Figure 10-6. You can also change the look of the text in the Over and Down button states if you want to give the button a rollover effect.

Figure 10-6. Creating the button

3. As you see when you move this project into Flash Builder, effective naming of the components makes the process move more efficiently later. Name the layer that the button is on redButtonLayer. Note that in the library, this button has been named automatically using the following convention; *layerName+ComponentType*. In this case, because the layer the button was originally on was named red, the button in the library is named redButton.

Next, you want to create the Data List component that is at the heart of this application. The elements to create the repeated item of the Data List are already on the stage (see Figure 10-7).

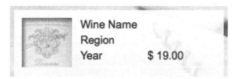

Figure 10-7. Elements of the Data List repeated item

4. Select all the elements to make up one wine listing (the thumbnail image, the four text boxes, and the line) by clicking each while holding down the Shift key.

5. Convert them into a Data List by selecting Convert Artwork to Component ➤ Data List in the HUD, as shown in Figure 10-8.

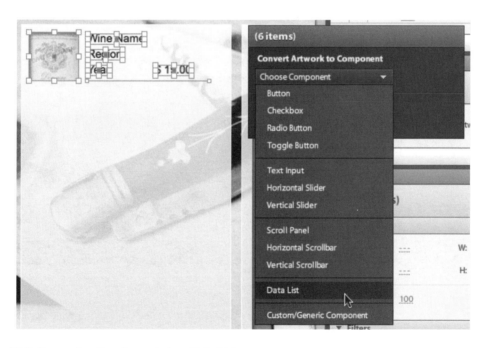

Figure 10-8. Converting the elements to a Data List

6. As you saw in Chapter 7, the Data List needs to know which pieces are to be repeated. This process is guided by the HUD. In the HUD, select Edit Parts (see Figure 10-9).

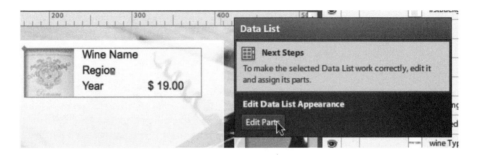

Figure 10-9. Editing the Data List's parts

7. In the Data List, select all the items again by clicking them while holding down the Shift key, and define them as the repeated item (see Figure 10-10).

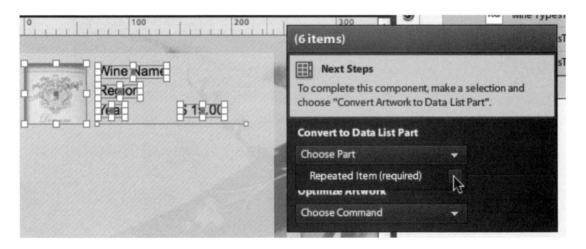

Figure 10-10. All the elements of the Data List set as a repeated item

8. Scale the Data List bounding box so the Data List occupies the whole of the white box it's on (see Figure 10-11).

Figure 10-11. Extending the bounding box

9. Because there will be more wines to present than the default five repeated items that are created in a Data List, add several more repeated items. To do so, add rows in the Design-Time Data panel, as shown in Figure 10-12. Because you'll add a vertical scrollbar to this Data List, you can add more rows than are visible at one time.

	Image 1	Text 1	Text 2	Text
0		Wine Name	Region	Year
1		Wine Name	Region	Year
2		Wine Name	Region	Year
3		Wine Name	Region	Year
4		Wine Name	Region	Year

+ Add Row

Figure 10-12. Design-Time Data panel for the Data List

10. It's important to have clear and consistent naming in the project. Notice that the naming of the repeated items is currently generic (image 1, Text 1, Text 2, and so on). These names give the developer little indication as to what needs to go in these fields. To make the names more meaningful, enter the Data List by double-clicking it; then, enter the repeated item, again by double-clicking. Here, rename the layers as shown in Figure 10-13.

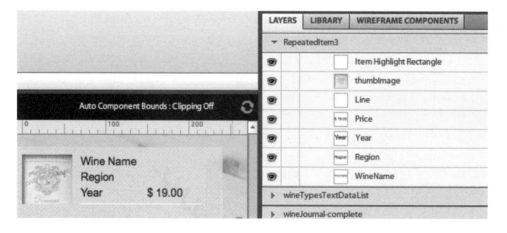

Figure 10-13. Renamed layers of the repeated item

Adding a Custom Vertical Scrollbar

You saw in Chapter 7 how to add a vertical scrollbar to a Data List. At the time, you used a wireframe component to see how this process works. In this example, a wireframe vertical scrollbar doesn't match the look of the rest of the application, so you need to create a vertical scrollbar with a custom look.

A vertical scrollbar is made up of four items: a *thumb* (the part the user moves), a *track* (on which the thumb moves), and, optionally, an up button and a down button. You can draw these in a graphics program and then convert them into a vertical scrollbar in Catalyst.

A design for a vertical scrollbar that matches the application's look is provided in the file verticalScrollBar.ai. This file consists of two rectangles (for the thumb and track) and two triangles (for the up and down buttons), as shown in Figure 10-14.

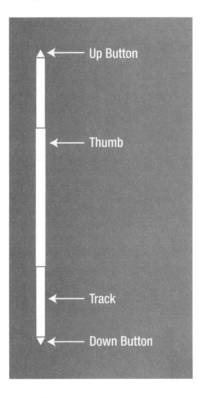

Figure 10-14. Artwork for the vertical scrollbar

If you aren't currently in the Data List component, double-click it to enter it. Then, follow these steps:

Import the Illustrator file (File ➤ Import ➤ Adobe Illustrator File (.ai)).

1. Select the Illustrator file, and use the default import settings. This places the image of the vertical scrollbar in the Data List (see Figure 10-15). Position the graphics so they're in the appropriate location for the scrollbar.

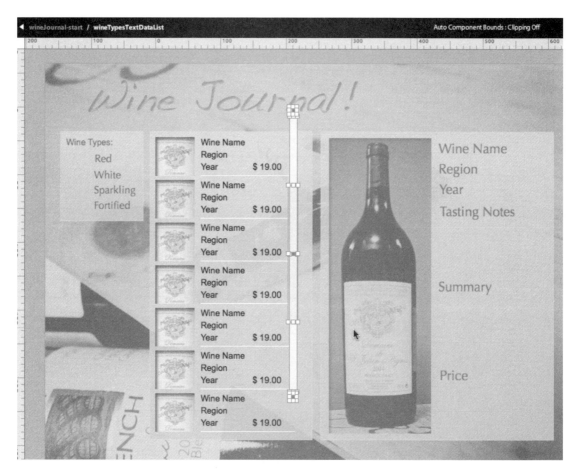

Figure 10-15. Importing the artwork for the vertical scrollbar

2. To make this artwork into a functioning scrollbar, with all the pieces still selected, choose Modify ➤ Convert Artwork to Component ➤ Vertical Scrollbar, as shown in Figure 10-16.

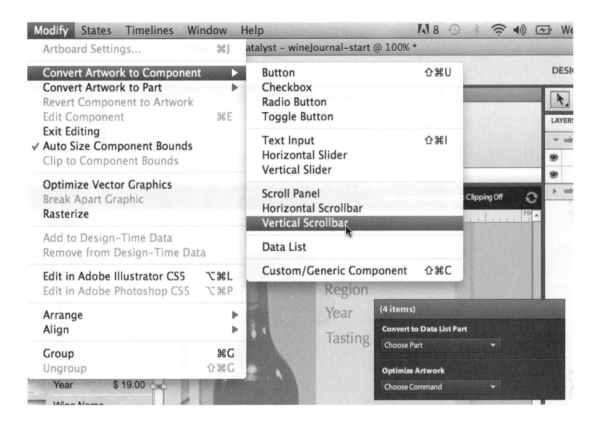

Figure 10-16. Artwork converted to a vertical scrollbar

3. Double-click the scrollbar to enter it so you can define which piece of the artwork becomes which part of the component. Select each part of the artwork and define its role in the HUD, as shown in Figure 10-17.

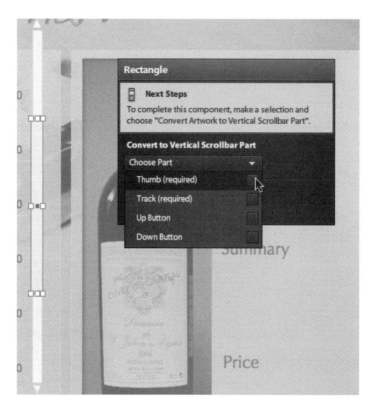

Figure 10-17. Defining the parts of the vertical scrollbar

With this, the vertical scrollbar is complete and functional. Run the project to see it in action. The vertical scrollbar now moves the repeated items in the Data List.

Adding the States

So far, you've created the application so that everything is visible at once. When the application is complete, you want the experience to be a bit different. At first, you want the user to see only the wine-type selection menu. When they click, you want the Data List to Appear. And finally, when the user selects one of the wines, the detailed information should become visible. To achieve this, you need to create two more states. Follow these steps:

1. Duplicate the Expanded state, and name it WineList (see Figure 10-18). This state presents the menu and the Data List but not the detailed information.

Figure 10-18. Duplicating the Expanded state to create the WineList state

2. To make the detailed information invisible, click the eye icon for the ExpandedInfo folder in the Layers panel (see Figure 10-19). Doing so makes all the elements that are part of the detailed information not visible in this state.

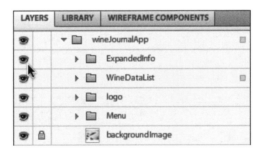

Figure 10-19. ExpandedInfo made invisible in the Layers panel

3. In the same way, you can create a duplicate state that shows only the wine-selection menu. Duplicate the WineList state, and name the copy selectionMenu. In this state, set the WineDataList folder to be invisible by selecting the eye icon. The design should now look like Figure 10-20.

Figure 10-20. Design of the selectionMenu state

4. To set this state as the first state the user sees, right-click the state and select Set as Default State from the context menu, as shown in Figure 10-21.

Figure 10-21. Defining selectionMenu as the default state

You now have the basic structure of the project complete. Next, you create the interactions to control the movement between states and then bring the project into Flash Builder to connect it to the outside data source.

Adding Interactions

To move the user through the different states of the application, you need to add interactions to the components you've created. The first of these is placed on the redButton. When the redButton is clicked, the application should transition to the WineList state. Follow these steps:

1. Select the redButton. In the Interactions panel, define the interaction as On Click ➤ Play Transition to State ➤ WineList (see Figure 10-22).

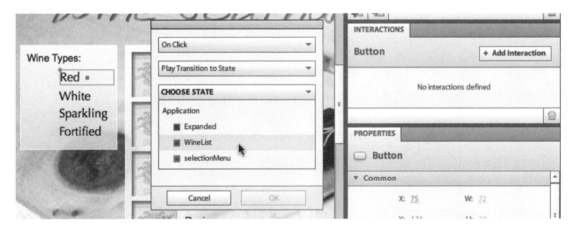

Figure 10-22. Adding an interaction to redButton

2. In a similar way, when the user selects one of the wines, you want the application to transition to the Expanded state that shows the detailed information about the wine. Select the WineDataList and, in the Interactions panel, define the interaction as On Select ➤ Play Transition to State ➤ Expanded (see Figure 10-23).

It doesn't matter in which state you define the interactions, because they're associated with the component, not the state.

3. Save the project (File ➤ Save).

The Catalyst part of this project is now finished. Next, you open the same project in Flash Builder; because Flash Builder can open a project created in Catalyst, nothing special needs to be done to make the project ready for import into Flash Builder.

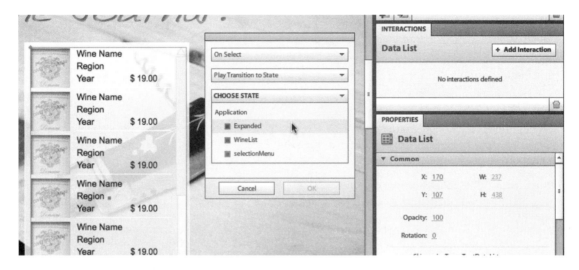

Figure 10-23. Adding an interaction to the Data List

Connecting the Application to Data in Flash Builder

Flash Builder is a developer-centric program that is used to create Rich Internet Applications (RIAs). Just like Catalyst, Flash Builder is part of the Flash Platform; thus the ultimate project that comes out of Flash Builder is a SWF file.

Flash Builder is a very data-friendly and powerful development environment. The purpose of this chapter is to see how a project goes from Flash Catalyst to Flash Builder, but you don't learn how to use Flash Builder itself—that's a subject for another book.

This chapter goes into developer territory, so don't get discouraged if the material is disorienting or unfamiliar. This isn't normally the part of the process that interaction designers are directly involved with, but seeing the entire process will help you understand how to better create the Catalyst files to make life easier for the developers.

After Flash Builder is installed on your computer, open it. Then, follow these steps:

1. In Flash Builder, import the Wine Journal Application that you created in Catalyst (File ➤ Import Flex Project (FXP)), as shown in Figure 10-24. Browse to the location of the file, and click Finish (see Figure 10-25).

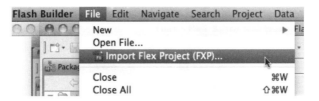

Figure 10-24. Importing the Catalyst project

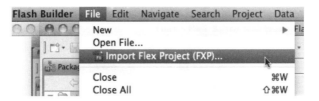

Figure 10-25. Import Flex Project dialog box

This brings your project into Flash Builder. You can see the project in the Package Explorer (see Figure 10-26).

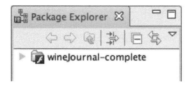

Figure 10-26. Project in the Package Explorer panel

A Flash Builder project is made up of a variety of files and folders that are all contained in a package. If you open the package by clicking the arrow next to the name, you can see its folders and files. The ones you're most concerned with are in the src folder. This is the Source folder, and it's automatically created to hold the project's main code files.

A package is essentially a collection of code. The default package holds the main code for the project. Main.mxml contains the main structure of the project you created in Catalyst, and the assets.images folder holds all the images you used. You can see these in Figure 10-27.

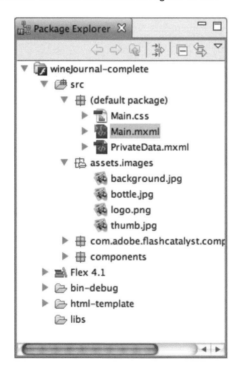

Figure 10-27. File structure of the project

2. Double-click `Main.mxml` to open the project in the code view. Click the Design button above the main window, as shown in Figure 10-28, to switch to the design view and get a more familiar look at your project.

```
Fb Start Page      Gm Main.mxml  ⊠
<∕> Source   📄 Design   Show state:   All states  ⬍
 1  <?xml version='1.0' encoding='UTF-8'?>
 2⊝ <s:Application xmlns:ATE="http://ns.adobe.com/ate/2009" xmlns:ai="http://ns.adobe.com/ai/2009" xml
 3      <fx:Style source="Main.css"/>
 4⊝     <fx:Script><![CDATA[
 5             ]]></fx:Script>
 6⊝     <s:states>
 7          <s:State fc:color="0xcc0000" name="Expanded"/>
 8          <s:State name="WineList"/>
 9          <s:State name="selectionMenu"/>
10      </s:states>
11⊝     <fx:DesignLayer d:id="2" d:userLabel="wineJournalApp">
12          <s:BitmapImage id="bitmapimage7" d:locked="true" smooth="true" source="@Embed('assets/imag
13⊝         <fx:DesignLayer d:userLabel="Menu">
14⊝             <s:Rect alpha="0.9" height="132" id="rect4" d:userLabel="menuBackgroundRectangle" widt
15⊝                 <s:stroke>
16                      <s:SolidColorStroke caps="none" color="#FFFFFF" joints="miter" miterLimit="4"
17                  </s:stroke>
18⊝                 <s:fill>
19⊝                     <s:LinearGradient rotation="90">
20                          <s:GradientEntry alpha="1" color="#FFFFFF" ratio="0"/>
21                          <s:GradientEntry alpha="1.0" color="0xE9E5DA" ratio="1"/>
22                      </s:LinearGradient>
23                  </s:fill>
24              </s:Rect>
25              <s:RichText color="#010101" fontFamily="Arial" fontSize="13" id="richtext11" tabStops
26              <s:RichText color="#010101" fontFamily="Optima" fontSize="16" id="labelDisplay1" tabS
27              <s:RichText color="#010101" fontFamily="Optima" fontSize="16" id="labelDisplay2" tabS
28              <s:RichText color="#010101" fontFamily="Optima" fontSize="16" id="labelDisplay3" tabS
29              <s:Button skinClass="components.redButton" x="75" y="131"/>
```

Figure 10-28. Code view of the project

In this project, you replace the data that is used to populate the list of wines. In Catalyst, the data was the single repeated wine that you used when you created the Data List. In a finished application, the data that populates the list comes from an outside file or database. In this case, you use data from an XML file—specifically, the provided file `XMLAndImages.zip`.

Because your data source is an XML file, you bring the file into the project so it's a part of the overall package. It's good form to bring the XML into the project's `assets` folder but keep it separate from the images. To do this, you need to create a new folder named `data` in the `assets` folder.

3. Right-click the `assets.images` folder, and select New ➤ Folder from the context menu as shown in Figure 10-29.

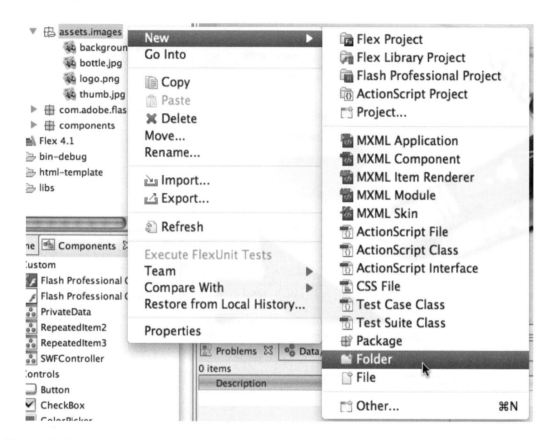

Figure 10-29. Adding a new folder for data

4. In the New Folder dialog box, select `assets`, give the folder the name `data`, and click Finish, as shown in Figure 10-30.

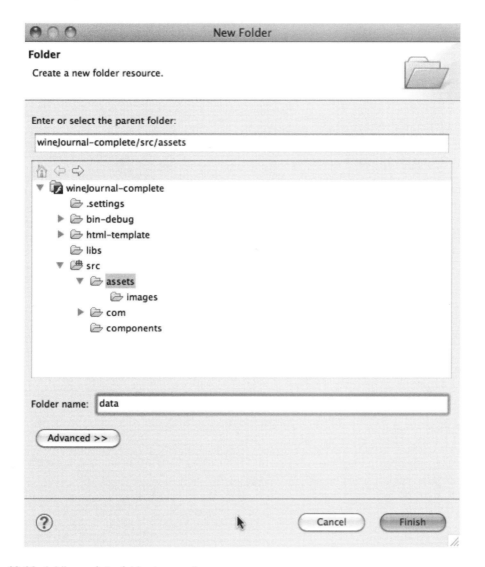

Figure 10-30. Adding a `data` folder to `assets`

5. The XML file and a series of images that are used for the different wines are provided with the example files for this chapter in the zip file `XMLAndImages.zip`. Download and extract these files onto your desktop.

6. To make the XML part of the project, drag and drop the file directly into the data folder in the Package Explorer panel, as shown in Figure 10-31. Doing so places a copy of the XML file into the assets folder; it will be exported with the project when it's finished.

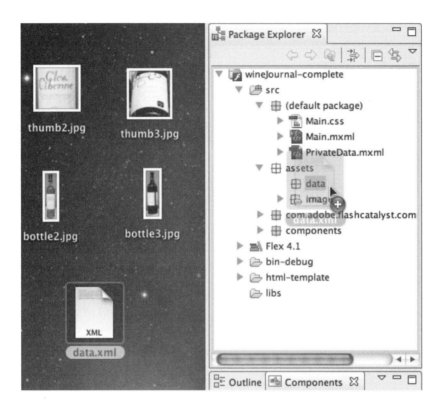

Figure 10-31. Dragging the XML file into the data folder

7. Do the same thing to make the images part of the project: drag the images that were in XMLAndImages.zip into the assets.images folder.

With the XML file in place, you can now make it into a data service in the project. A *data service* takes in and processes data, making the individual fields accessible later in this example. When you make the data into a data service, Flash Builder can connect or, in the language of Flash Builder, *bind* the information in the file to the individual components.

8. To create a data service, select the Data Services tab along the bottom panel, and click Connect to Data/Service, as shown in Figure 10-32. Doing so brings up a Data/Service wizard to guide you through the process (see Figure 10-33). As you can see, Flash Builder can work with a variety of different kinds of data sources.

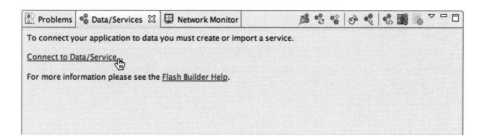

Figure 10-32. Data/Services panel

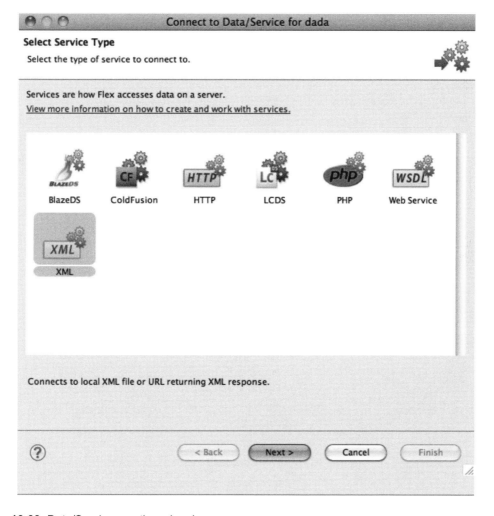

Figure 10-33. Data/Service creation wizard

9. Select XML, and click Next.

10. The next step in the wizard has you locate the XML file you need to use. To find the one you just added to the project, click Browse beside the Path field (see Figure 10-34). This opens the Browse window at the root of the current project.

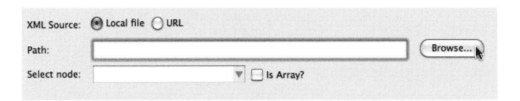

Figure 10-34. Path to the data service

11. Navigate through the project's file structure until you reach the `data.xml` file. It's in the `src/assets/data/` folder, as shown in Figure 10-35. Click Finish to complete the creation of the data service.

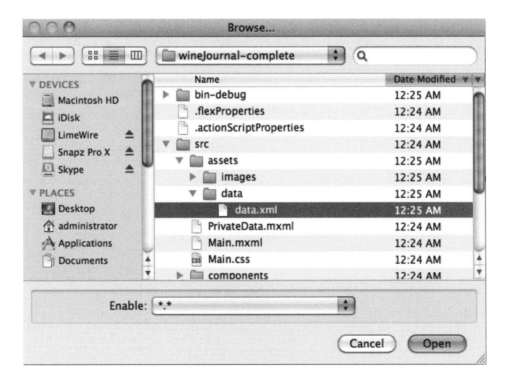

Figure 10-35. XML file selected in the project's folder structure

You've now created the data service. Flash Builder understands the structure of the XML, and it can be used to bind to a component. In the Data/Services panel, you can see the structure of the XML file, as shown in Figure 10-36.

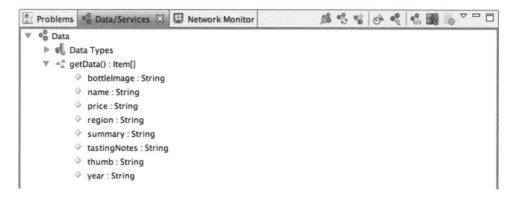

Figure 10-36. Structure of the XML file

12. You now want to connect the data service with the Data List you created in Catalyst. Select the WineList state in the States panel at upper-right in the interface (see Figure 10-37).

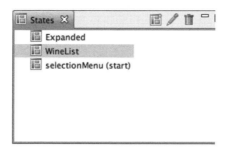

Figure 10-37. Selecting the WineList state in the States panel

Notice that when the Data List is selected, an icon that looks like a chain appears to the left of the component. This is the binding icon (see Figure 10-38). Click it to bind the data service to the component.

Figure 10-38. Binding icon

13. You receive a message stating the component is already bound (see Figure 10-39). This is because the Data List has been bound, in Catalyst, to the design-time data. Because you no longer want to use the design-time data, you can replace the binding. Click OK in the message.

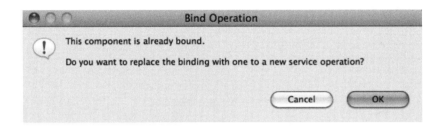

Figure 10-39. Message regarding a preexisting binding

14. The next dialog box gives you some control over how the data service binds to the Data List (see Figure 10-40). Keep the default settings, and click OK.

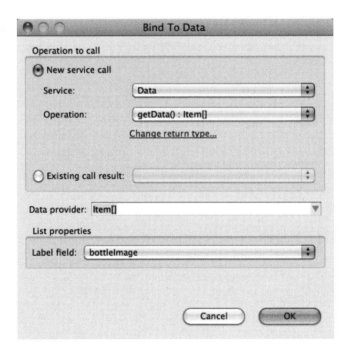

Figure 10-40. Bind to Data dialog box

The contents of the Data List disappear at this point. This is because, although the data from the XML file is now being passed to the Data List, it doesn't yet know how to handle the data. It doesn't know which field from the XML goes into which part of the repeated item. You need to manually connect this directly in the code.

All the components that you created in Catalyst also exist in Flash Builder as individual MXML files. These MXML files control the appearance of the individual components and can be found in the Package Explorer panel in the `src/components` folder, as shown in Figure 10-41.

Figure 10-41. Component MXML files in the Package Explorer panel

The component you're concerned with here is RepeatedItem. This is the part of the Data List that is repeated for each wine.

15. Double-click the `RepeatedItem.mxml` file to open it. It isn't much to look at in the design view, because it doesn't contain the data. But if you switch to source view, you can see the code that makes up the component.

This source view can be difficult to understand if you aren't familiar with MXML, but it holds all the properties of the components you created in Catalyst (see Figure 10-42). You need to make a few small changes to this code in order for it to understand how to handle the data that is coming in.

Let's start with the thumb image of the wine label. This can be found at line 17 (see Figure 10-43). The `source` property of this image defines where the image data comes from. Right now, it's looking for a field called `image1` in the XML file, because this was the generic name given it from the design-time data. This is represented as `source="{data.image1}"`. You need to change it to the correct field in the XML: `thumb`.

Figure 10-42. Code View for RepeatedItem

Figure 10-43. MXML for the thumb image

16. Change the `source` property to `{data.thumb}`, as shown in Figure 10-44.

Figure 10-44. Thumb image connected to the correct data field from XML

In the same way, the text field that contains the information about the wine name, region, year, and price needs to be pointed to the correct part of the XML file. You can find these components at lines 8 to 11. Currently, the data fields they're pulling from are named `{data.text1}`, `{data.text2}`, `{data.text3}`, and `{data.text4}`, as shown in Figure 10-45.

Figure 10-45. MXML for the text components

You need to change these to pull from the appropriate fields. You can tell which data should go to which component by looking at the `userLabel` field of each component. These are the names of the layers you added in Catalyst. (You can tell that this process would be considerably more difficult if the userLabel field weren't clear.)

17. Change the fields to {data.name}, {data.region}, {data.year}, and {data.price}, as shown in Figure 10-46.

```
<s:RichText color="#010101" fontFamily="Arial" fontSize="13" id="richtext0" tabStops="S0 S50" text="{data.name}" d:userLabel="WineName" x="70"
<s:RichText color="#010101" fontFamily="Arial" fontSize="13" id="richtext6" tabStops="S0 S50" text="{data.region}" d:userLabel="Region" x="70"
<s:RichText color="#010101" fontFamily="Arial" fontSize="13" id="richtext7" tabStops="S0 S50" text="{data.year}" d:userLabel="Year" x="70" y="
<s:RichText color="#010101" fontFamily="Arial" fontSize="13" id="richtext8" tabStops="S0 S50" text="{data.price}" d:userLabel="Price" x="150"
```

Figure 10-46. Text components connected to the correct data fields from XML

That's all for the Data List. To see the project in action, run it by selecting Run ➤ Run Main in the main menu (see Figure 10-47).

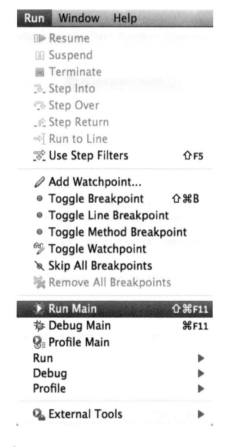

Figure 10-47. Running the project

The contents of the Data List showing all the wines are now brought in from the XML data, as shown in Figure 10-48. Any future changes in the XML file will be reflected in the contents of the Data List.

Figure 10-48. Data List with data coming in from XML

Clicking any of the wines in the Data List still bring up the detailed view. This information is still static. Making it live would require a deeper investigation of the coding in Flash Builder than is in the scope of this book, but you should now have some idea of how you might go about it.

18. There is a bit of an issue: when you click the Data List, it seems to disappear (see Figure 10-49). To prevent this, select the Data List in the `Main.mxml` file (in the design view), and select Apply Current Properties to All States from the context menu (see Figure 10-50). This carries over the changes that you made to the Expanded state.

Figure 10-49. Issue with the Data List

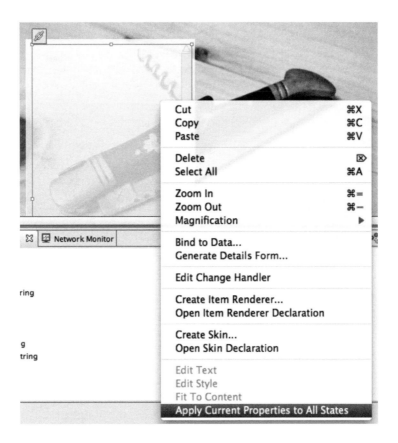

Figure 10-50. Applying properties to all states to eliminate the issue

Conclusion

You now see how one piece of a design is connected to an outside data source. The development process continues from here to bind more of the components to the data, but this example gives you an overall sense of how the process works.

As you can see in this example, the developer works with the same file and with the same images in Flash Builder that you use in Flash Catalyst. This means ambiguously named components and uncompressed images stay with the project after you hand it over, making it more difficult to work with and slower to download. Taking care of naming and image compression in Catalyst makes the project an easier file to work with.

The final point to keep in mind as you finish this book is that the real power of Catalyst lies in changing your design process to make you a better interaction designer. With Catalyst, you can design a prototype much more quickly, and this should lead you to create many more prototypes. Use this speed to sketch the interaction, experiment with different approaches, and not rely on your first idea about a design.

This concludes the book. We hope you've found it useful, and we look forward to seeing the work you produce with it.

Index

You Need the Companion eBook

Your purchase of this book entitles you to buy the companion PDF-version eBook for only $10. Take the weightless companion with you anywhere.

We believe this Apress title will prove so indispensable that you'll want to carry it with you everywhere, which is why we are offering the companion eBook (in PDF format) for $10 to customers who purchase this book now. Convenient and fully searchable, the PDF version of any content-rich, page-heavy Apress book makes a valuable addition to your programming library. You can easily find and copy code—or perform examples by quickly toggling between instructions and the application. Even simultaneously tackling a donut, diet soda, and complex code becomes simplified with hands-free eBooks!

Once you purchase your book, getting the $10 companion eBook is simple:

1. Visit **www.apress.com/promo/tendollars/**.

2. Complete a basic registration form to receive a randomly generated question about this title.

3. Answer the question correctly in 60 seconds, and you will receive a promotional code to redeem for the $10.00 eBook.

233 Spring Street, New York, NY 10013

Offer valid through 4/11.